● Navigating Power: A Rulebook Series

SHADOWS OF AUTHORITY
RULE #1 - NEVER OUTSHINE

Dive into the intrigue of power dynamics and historical secrets, exploring the art of subtle influence that shapes personal and political destinies.

Table Of Contents

The Origins of Subtle Influence

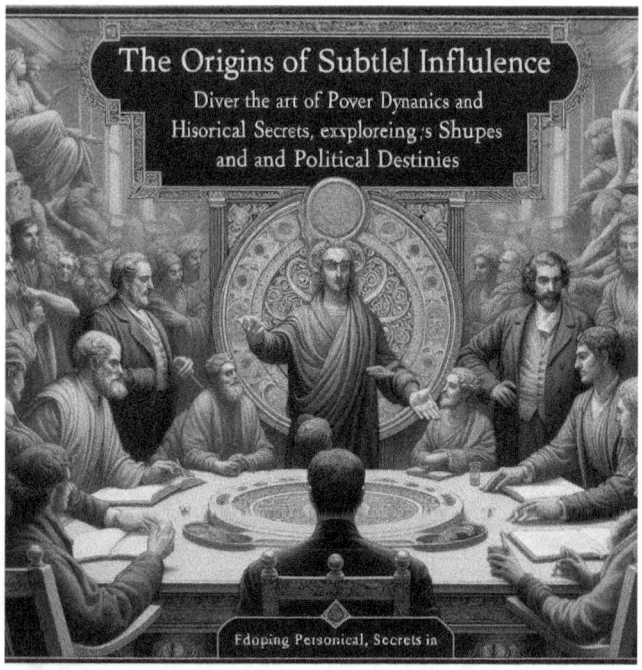

Throughout human history, the dance of power has been a complicated and enthralling display. From the corridors of ancient empires to the hallowed halls of modern governance, the skill of wielding influence has played a defining role in determining the fates of individuals and nations alike. At the center of this age-old search is a subtle expertise, an elusive skill that goes beyond raw power and overt authority: the art of subtle influence.

To understand the origins of this clandestine procedure, one needs to travel deep into antiquity, where the seeds of manipulation and diplomacy were planted. Long before the ink dried on the pages of written history, crafty minds were busy creating webs of influence that would withstand the test of time.

With the advent of civilization came the knowledge that power, in its most basic form, might be a double-edged blade. Those who wielded it with a heavy hand frequently faced opposition and insurrection. During these early epochs, perceptive individuals began to grasp the strength of a more refined approach—the power of suggestion, the appeal of secrecy, and the mystique of influence conducted in the background.

In the expansive courts of ancient empires, where kings and queens ruled vast lands, advisors murmured advice that was as subtle as it was effective. The clever among them understood the main rule: never outshine the monarch. This notion, distilled into the first rule of power, established the foundation of the delicate dance between advisors and monarchs, paving the way for the sophisticated art of subtle persuasion.

As cultures changed, so did the tactics for wielding influence. The political landscape of ancient Greece, for example, attested to the rhetorical prowess of orators like Demosthenes, who could alter public opinion with the cadence of their words alone. The Romans, with their complex web of familial and political relationships, took the game of subtle influence to new heights.

Across Asia, from Chinese imperial courts to Indian maharajas, the delicate dance of diplomacy expressed the art of subtle persuasion. The exchange of gifts, the building of alliances, and the manipulation of information were tools in the hands of individuals attempting to negotiate the complex web of power relations.

The medieval courts of Europe, with their knights, ladies, and cunning aristocracy, were theaters of intrigue where subtle influence was elevated to an art form. In his landmark work "The Prince," Machiavelli outlined the ideas of cunning administration, emphasizing the significance of maintaining the appearance of virtue while manipulating events subtly.

As the decades passed, the concept of subtle influence spread beyond the bounds of royal courts and into every strata of society. The rise of modern democracies did not reduce their importance; rather, they adapted to changing circumstances. Individuals continued to perfect the art of shaping destinies through the delicate orchestration of influence in business boardrooms, academic halls, and political chambers.

"The Shadows of Authority Rule #1: Never Outshine" takes you on a fascinating trip through the past, revealing historical mysteries and undiscovered anecdotes about the beginnings of subtle influence. Join us as we journey into the labyrinthine hallways of power, where shadows dance and authority whispers the eternal norms of engagement.

The Conventional Wisdom on Persuasion
Throughout human history, the skill of persuasion has been crucial in determining the paths taken by individuals, groups, and countries. From the ancient Egyptian and

Mesopotamian civilizations to the European royal courts and Eastern intellectual traditions, people have used subtle influence to maneuver through the complex dance between authority and power.

Persuasion's Origins

Persuasion has its roots in the earliest human communities, when people discovered they could influence others to accomplish their objectives. The skill of rhetoric developed as a potent instrument for persuasion in ancient Greece. Prominent speakers like Aristotle and Cicero developed their persuasive talents by realizing how crucial it is to appeal to credibility, reason, and feelings in order to change people's minds.

The Influence of Speech

In the intricate fabric of power, where shadows of authority reign and the unspoken exerts more sway than the spoken, mastery of speech becomes a powerful weapon. In the halls of power, Rule #1 rings true: never outshine. Speech's influence is an art form, a delicate dance between the uttered and the unspoken, a symphony that molds destiny and affects history.

Words, like silent warriors, have the power to both build and destroy empires. Within the enigmatic domain of subtle influence, cadence, tone, and word choice become instruments to be played with finesse by those who realize the power they possess. Each sentence is a brushstroke on the canvas of perception, creating pictures of power or fragility, trust or mistrust.

As characters negotiate the complexities of political landscapes and personal desires, the spoken word becomes a double-edged sword. It can form coalitions, plant seeds of conflict, incite revolutions, or calm unrest. In the shadows, where authority casts silent spells, the impact of speech lasts far beyond the present moment, reverberating down the corridors of time.

The protagonist, a master of rhetoric, navigates the hazardous waters of power dynamics, using words not only to communicate but also to manipulate. The delicate intricacies of language, the implicit agreements within the grammar of silence, and the strategic pauses between sentences all help to orchestrate influence.

In the sacred halls of historical secrets, where echoes of the past reverberate, the protagonists discover the hidden power of oratory skill. Ancient texts reveal lost speeches that persuaded nations, while dusty archives contain the whispered confessions of powerful figures whose carefully planned words altered the destiny of civilizations.

The study of the impact of speech extends beyond the individual, delving into the collective psyche of cultures influenced by the resonance of eloquence. Public speeches, private meetings, and clandestine negotiations become watershed events in the story as the protagonists navigate the perilous waters of words to impose authority or elicit cooperation.

As the story progresses, the characters wrestle with the moral implications of linguistic manipulation, challenging the ethical boundaries of the shadows they cast. The conflict between using speech as a tool for enlightenment and as a cover for deception becomes a central topic, forcing the characters to face the repercussions of their linguistic choices.

In "Shadows of Authority Rule #1: Never Outshine," the investigation of the influence of speech provides a riveting prism through which readers may watch the ebb and flow of power, the delicate dance of personalities, and the developing drama of historical secrets. The art of subtle influence, portrayed through words, becomes a narrative thread that weaves together the tapestry of intrigue, enthralling readers with the shadows that form both personal and political destinies.

The Craft of Disguise

Although persuasiveness has the potential to bring about good, it can also be used for evil. Known as "Machiavellianism" after the political philosopher Niccolò Machiavelli, the idea originated in ancient Rome. In "The Prince," Machiavelli examined the brutal methods used by tyrants to hold onto and strengthen their position of authority. His writings explored the art of manipulation, stressing the value of trickery, shrewdness, and the calculated use of terror to further one's goals.

The Court's Intrigues
The European courts developed into hubs of deft political maneuvering and subtly exerted power during the Renaissance. Courtly intrigue was a skill that individuals like Cardinal Richelieu and Catherine de'Medici perfected, utilizing their charm and cunning to control everyone around them. They were able to secure their positions of power and reshape the political environment through their well-considered activities.

The Eastern Wisdom

In the sacred corridors of ancient Eastern civilizations, where the air was thick with the aroma of exotic spices and sages' wisdom echoed through time, there was a profound grasp of the delicate dance between power and finesse. The Shadows of Authority, a clandestine and venerated group, guarded this arcane knowledge, passing down its secrets from generation to generation.

As the sun fell below the horizon, throwing long shadows across elegant palaces and peaceful temples, the Shadows of Authority congregated in dimly lit chambers where secrets were traded like valuable gems. In these clandestine gatherings, the sages conveyed Rule #1, "Never Outshine," a motto that spanned centuries and became woven into the very fabric of Eastern philosophy.

To the uninitiated, this principle may appear paradoxical—a paradox in a culture that frequently honors the brave and smart. However, those who went into the complicated tapestry of power dynamics discovered a golden thread that held the key to unlocking the mysteries of influence and control.

The Shadows of Authority, masters of the subtle arts, saw that genuine power resided not in the dazzling light of one's achievements but in the strategic use of shadows. They discovered the capacity to mold destinies and manipulate the path of history by dancing with subtlety.

The concept that people seeking to lead must do so with quiet strength, like a river that transforms the terrain over time, eroding obstacles without declaring its existence, was central to Eastern knowledge. The Shadows taught that individuals who embraced the shadows might travel through the world with unmatched grace, avoiding the traps that awaited those who sought the spotlight.

As students of this ancient wisdom, the Shadows of Authority evolved into influence architects capable of navigating the complex web of human interactions and political landscapes. They recognized that true authority was not wielded with a hard hand but rather manifested in the skillful orchestration of events, leading others to feel they held the reins while the true puppeteer went unnoticed.

The Shadows' ancient secrets were more than just archives of forgotten tales; they were real, breathing stories that unfolded in the darkest corners of power. From the imperial courts of long-gone empires to the meditation chambers of secluded mystics, the echoes of Rule #1 rang out, warning everyone who dared to explore the shadows that true authority resided in the mastery of subtlety.

As the moon rose to its zenith, casting a silvery glow over the landscapes where empires rose and fell, the Shadows of Authority maintained their timeless vigil, ensuring that the delicate balance of power and subtlety remained an enduring legacy for those seeking to comprehend the Shadows of Authority.

The   Lasting   Trajectories

Persuasion is an age-old skill that nevertheless has an impact on modern society. People who are aware of the subtleties of influence can succeed in both the political and corporate spheres by navigating intricate power dynamics. Through examining the methods and approaches utilized by notable historical personalities, we can acquire an understanding of the ageless concepts that dictate human communication.

We will go deeper into the nuances of subtle influence in the ensuing chapters, covering topics such as the psychology of power, the skill of observation, strategic communication, and navigating power systems. We'll look at case studies of powerful people from history, evaluating their strategies and breaking down the moral dilemmas that come with using persuasion. Lastly, we will look at how subtle influence is used in daily life, including in the workplace, personal relationships, and other settings.

Come along on this insightful adventure with us as we solve the mysteries of the shadows and discover how to effectively use subtle influence.

Machiavelli's Skillful Trickery

Machiavelli's name echoes through history like a whispered secret in the dimly lit corridors of power, where shadows dance and authority is hidden. His sharp mind, acute observations, and unapologetic embrace of political strategy have left an indelible imprint on the global knowledge of power dynamics. The echoes of his teachings, captured in "The Prince," have become a timeless guide for those attempting to traverse the complex landscape of influence.

As we delve into the heart of "Shadows of Authority Rule #1—Never Outshine," it is critical to understand the complexities of Machiavelli's cunning deceit. At the heart of his ideology is a profound grasp of the human condition, which recognizes that power is a dynamic, ever-shifting reality that necessitates strategic mastery.

Machiavelli's essay, published in the early 16th century, transcends its temporal context, providing insights that are startlingly applicable in the modern world. His examination of the delicate balance between morality and vice, compassion and ruthlessness, reveals a tapestry of nuances that control the actions of those in positions of authority. It is a lesson in pragmatism, recognizing that the quest for and maintenance of power frequently necessitates a departure from normal moral principles.

In the chapters of "Shadows of Authority," Machiavelli's lessons become a tapestry on which characters weave their fates. The book's fundamental concept, the art of subtle persuasion, may be traced back to the Florentine diplomat's strategic finesse. Characters struggle with the contradiction of virtue and necessity, dealing with the shadows of their own desires as they navigate a world where alliances are established in whispers and severed in silence.

Machiavelli's deceit consists not only in the overt exercise of power but also in the deliberate manipulation of perception. He recognized that the ruler's image is just as important as the physical authority they hold. The finesse with which one impacts perception, creating a character that commands respect and dread, is a skill that echoes through the hallways of political intrigue in "Shadows of Authority."

As the story progresses, readers will see people use Machiavellian techniques to outmaneuver opponents and protect their places in a world with high stakes and devastating repercussions. The book looks into the psychological underpinnings of power, examining the delicate dance between ruler and ruler, puppeteer and puppet.

In the shadows of Machiavelli's wisdom, the protagonists in "Shadows of Authority Rule #1: Never Outshine" navigate a terrain where every gesture, every word, is a strategic move on the power chessboard. As we dive deeper into this realm of political intrigue and historical secrets, we are reminded that the echoes of Machiavelli's cunning deceit continue to resonate through the halls of authority, molding destinies and leaving an indelible impression on the tapestry of human history.

The Prince: A Guide to Subliminal Persuasion

Few names in history inspire as much curiosity and debate as Niccolò Machiavelli. Machiavelli was a well-known political philosopher, writer, and diplomat who was born in Florence, Italy, in 1469. Published in 1532, his most well-known piece of writing, "The Prince," is still regarded as a classic on the craft of subtly influencing others.

"The Prince" is a treatise on leadership and political power that gives rulers helpful guidance on acquiring and retaining power. Machiavelli's writings are essential reading for anybody studying political theory because of his understanding of the nature of power and the tactics needed to use it.

A Pragmatic Approach to Machiavelli's The Ends Justify the Means

Machiavelli had a pragmatic and unrepentant attitude toward power. He thought that in order to accomplish their objectives, rulers should be prepared to use any means, even if such measures raised ethical concerns. One of the most well-known expressions of this idea is "the ends justify the means."

Machiavelli believed that in order to preserve power, a ruler had to be prepared to behave brutally when required, resorting to violence, deceit, and manipulation. He maintained that since terror guarantees devotion and obedience, it is preferable to be feared than loved. Unlike many of his contemporaries, Machiavelli placed more emphasis on the pragmatic realities of power than on moral considerations.

The Craft of Trickery: Machiavelli's Tactics

In "The Prince," Machiavelli describes a variety of tactics that tyrants can use to subtly sway their people. Among these tactics are:

Sustaining Appearances: Despite their less than honorable behind-the-scenes activities, Machiavelli counsels kings to present an image of righteousness and morality. Leaders can win over their citizens' trust and support by projecting an image of virtue.

Divide and Conquer: According to Machiavelli, in order to reduce any resistance, rulers should take advantage of divisions among their subjects. Leaders can keep control and prevent the formation of a unified front opposing their authority by fostering conflict and playing several factions against one another.

Machiavelli places a strong emphasis on the necessity of managing the flow of information. Leaders have the ability to strategically sway public opinion and manipulate perceptions by carefully controlling the information that is released and to whom.

Machiavelli suggests that kings and queens surround themselves with obedient and capable counsel. These counselors must be dependable confidants who can offer insightful advice and assist the ruler in navigating the challenges of authority.

Changing with the Times: Machiavelli emphasizes the value of adaptability and flexibility. Leaders need to be flexible enough to adjust their plans and techniques as needed in order to constantly stay one step ahead of their rivals.

Machiavelli's Legacy: The Influence of "The Prince"

"The Prince" has influenced political theory and historical leaders' tactics in significant ways. Machiavelli's writings have been both respected and despised because of his emphasis on the practical realities of power, his acceptance of deceit and manipulation, and his belief that the objectives justify the means.

Some contend that Machiavelli's insights into the nature of power and the tactics needed to wield it effectively are crucial for leaders in a complex and competitive society, while others see him as a brutal and immoral thinker. Whatever one's stance, Machiavelli's writings have had a lasting impact on the skill of subliminal manipulation.

In the ensuing chapters, we shall examine several historical personalities who have perfected the skill of subtly influencing others; each will provide distinct viewpoints and methods. Readers will obtain important insights into the complex dance of power and influence by examining their strategies and comprehending the ideas that support their achievements. So let us go deeper into the shadows, where we will find the art of nuanced influence.

The Intrigues of the Court: A Renaissance Perspective

In the colorful tapestry of the Renaissance era, when art, culture, and intelligence blossomed, Europe's courts were not only epicenters of power but also crucibles of intrigue and subtlety. The air was dense with political intrigue, whispered alliances, and the covert dance of power. It was a time when the delicate balance of power was maintained not only by military force or economic prowess but also through the exquisite mastery of courtly maneuvers, with every gesture, word, and sidelong glance having the potential to influence the fates of individuals and nations alike.

In the magnificent halls filled with frescoes and gilded decorations, courtiers moved with grace and precision, negotiating the intricate web of alliances and rivalries that marked the time. The monarchs and their courts were more than just patrons of the arts; they were participants in a complex game of thrones, with the stakes being nothing less than the fate of countries.

The Shadows of Authority wield power in these courts, following Rule #1: Never Outshine. This unwritten rule regulated the actions of individuals who recognized that ultimate power rested not in flamboyant demonstrations but in the subtle manipulation of perception. The shadows were a haven for those who knew the art of nuance, where those wielding power became virtuosos in the symphony of whispers that rang through the halls of authority.

The courtiers, like excellent chess players, planned their moves with precision. Every grin had layers of significance, every partnership was a strategic play, and every bit of information was a pawn in a larger game. Diplomacy unfolded with the grace of a well-choreographed ballet, with a misstep resulting in political disaster.

Secrets were currency in Renaissance courts, and the Shadows of Authority served as clandestine brokers. Hidden chambers beneath tapestries, coded communications disguised as polite conversation, and the constant possibility of betrayal kept the environment tense. To traverse these perilous waters, one needed a deep understanding of the delicate dance of power, where loyalty was a rare diamond and trust was a fleeting illusion.

The art of subtle influence reached its pinnacle during this time, when courtiers refined their abilities in eloquence, diplomacy, and the delicate dance of flattery. Advisors whispered wise wisdom behind closed doors, while shadowy characters twisted power strings behind the thrones. The Renaissance courts became crucibles of political savvy when intelligence and cunning triumphed over raw power.

As we explore the Shadows of Authority from a Renaissance viewpoint, we unravel the tapestry of courtly intrigues, revealing carefully hidden truths and demonstrating the delicate balance that supported the era's splendor. It is a voyage into the heart of power, where shadows danced on the walls of authority, casting a silhouette that altered the course of history.

The Renaissance Court: A Center of Power
The Renaissance court was the focus of political, social, and cultural life during this period of history. It was a venue where monarchs, lords, and powerful persons gathered to proclaim their dominance, display their money, and participate in sophisticated power maneuvers. The court was not simply a physical site but also a complicated network of relationships, conflicts, and alliances that

altered the course of history.

The Art of Flattery and Subtle Influence

In the clandestine domain where shadows dance with authority, one rule reigns supreme: the first and greatest commandment of power play, "Never Outshine." It's a delicate dance of manipulation and subtlety, a game played in the halls of power where every step counts and every word is a brushstroke on the canvas of destiny. Welcome to the fascinating world of subtle influence, where the skill of flattery is the key to accessing hidden levels of power.

Flattery, when used correctly, becomes a powerful weapon in the arsenal of individuals who understand the delicate fabric of human behavior. It is an art and a craft that crosses time and cultures, weaving its way through history. From the courts of ancient kings to modern-day boardrooms, the dance of flattery has sculpted destinies and brought down empires.

Flattery is fundamentally the art of crafting compliments that speak to the recipient's deepest wishes and insecurities. It's a delicate blend of honesty and manipulation, a nuanced dance that elevates both parties while keeping them unaware of the strings being tugged behind the scenes.

The books of history are littered with brilliant manipulators who grasped the subtle art of flattery. Cleopatra, the Queen of Egypt, captivated Julius Caesar and Mark Antony with her silver-tongued allure, employing flattery to ensure her kingdom's success. Machiavelli, in his treatise "The Prince," extolled the advantages of flattery, recommending the use of praise to acquire favor and influence.

Flattery reigns supreme in the vast theater of politics, with politicians and statesmen constantly exchanging praises and accolades. From diplomatic etiquette to carefully crafted speeches, the political environment fosters the art of flattery. A charismatic leader who can build a narrative that appeals to the populace while discreetly charming those in power becomes a master puppeteer in the vast spectacle of governing.

However, the art of flattery is not limited to the corridors of power alone. In personal interactions, it is the silent power that forges connections and strengthens bonds. Friends flatter friends, lovers flatter lovers, and in the complex web of human connections, the subtle dance of compliments serves as the glue that holds hearts and minds together.

Understanding the art of flattery entails discovering the secrets of influence and persuasion. It is to acknowledge that power is not necessarily wielded harshly but can be beautifully managed with subtle strokes of appreciation. As we go deeper into the shadows of authority, let us consider the intricacies of flattery and the enormous effect it has on the ebb and flow of personal and political fortunes.

In the next chapters, we shall examine the anatomy of flattery, including its various forms and expressions. We will investigate the psychology behind the allure of compliments and decipher the hidden messages included in seemingly innocent phrases. Join me on this voyage into the heart of the art of flattery and subtle influence, where the shadows of authority strike a spell on those who dare to walk the delicate path of power dynamics and historic secrets.

The Role of Patronage

Patronage played a vital part in the Renaissance court, with wealthy individuals providing financial support and security to artists, writers, and intellectuals. In return, these patrons wanted devotion and influence over the creative output of their proteges. The relationship between patron and artist was often a delicate dance, with both parties striving to maximize their own interests while maintaining the illusion of mutual respect and admiration.

The Power of Intrigue and Secrecy
Intrigue and concealment were the currency of the Renaissance court. Behind the grandeur and splendor of the courtly life, there were secret motives, whispered chats, and clandestine meetings. Those who desired to wield power had to be proficient at navigating this world of secrets and whispers, carefully choosing their confidants and allies while guarding their own objectives.

The Role of Women in Courtly Intrigues
While the Renaissance court was frequently dominated by men, women played a crucial role in courtly intrigues. Queens, princesses, and noblewomen used their attractiveness, wit, and political acumen to exercise influence on the men in their lives. They were often the power behind the throne, pulling the strings from the shadows and dictating the course of history.

The Legacy of Renaissance Courts
The intrigues of the Renaissance court continue to grab our imagination and impact our understanding of power relations. The

lessons learnt from this age are still pertinent today, reminding us of the timeless nature of human ambition, manipulation, and the quest of influence. By examining the methods adopted by historical people in the courts of the Renaissance, we can obtain significant insights into the art of subtle persuasion and apply them to our own lives and interactions.

In the next chapter, we will go deeper into the power dynamics that support subtle influence, investigating the hierarchical structures, psychological elements, and perceptual biases that shape our interactions and impact the success of our influence efforts.

The Subtle Power of Eastern Philosophies
In the shadows of authority, where the delicate dance of power plays takes place, Eastern ideologies have had a significant influence. In terms of political maneuvering, personal rising, and historical shaping, Eastern knowledge has cast a subtle yet persistent spell. This enchantment, founded on centuries-old ideas and teachings, has permeated the fabric of societies and civilizations, leaving an indelible imprint on the art of governing and the delicate tapestry of human interactions.

The concept of harmony is central to Eastern philosophies, as it strives to balance competing energies. The ancient traditions of Confucianism, Taoism, and Buddhism presented a sophisticated knowledge of power relations, emphasizing the importance of balance and the interconnection of everything. These ideologies, which originated in the ancient civilizations of China, India, and Japan, foster a deep awareness of the nuances that underpin the exercise of authority.

Confucianism, with its emphasis on moral purity and social harmony, directs the holder of power toward good government. Confucius' wise guidance reverberates through the ages, reminding leaders of the value of ethical behavior, empathy, and the cultivation of personal integrity. "Rule #1: Never Outshine" is echoed in Confucian teachings, urging individuals in positions of leadership to utilize their power with humility and a clear awareness of the influence their actions may have on the complex web of societal ties.

Taoism, on the other hand, introduces the concept of Wu Wei, or the art of effortless action. It empowers leaders to handle power dynamics with fluidity that goes beyond violent imposition. Lao Tzu, a Taoist sage, whispers in rulers' ears, telling them to set a good example and recognize the power that comes with giving instead of opposing. Leaders may discover power in the intricacy of non-action that extends beyond overt signs of dominance.

Buddhism, with its teachings on impermanence and the interconnectedness of existence, offers rulers a prism through which to examine the fleeting nature of power. Understanding that everything is constantly changing motivates leaders to value adaptability and foresight. The rule of not outshining becomes a strategic imperative, understanding the fleeting nature of any position of authority and the need for a controlled approach to influence.

The combination of these Eastern beliefs creates a unique perspective on power that goes beyond raw force and compulsion. Instead, it encourages leaders to manage the delicate dance of authority with wisdom, foresight, and a thorough awareness of the complex fabric of human connections.

As we dive into the shadows of authority, the subtle power of Eastern ideas shines as a guiding light, showing the route to a peaceful balance of power and governance. Through an examination of these ancient teachings, we discover the everlasting principles that continue to shape both personal and political destinies, weaving a tale of intrigue and enlightenment into the ever-changing epic of human history.

Taoism: The Way of Natural Influence
Taoism emphasizes the significance of aligning oneself with the natural flow of the cosmos, known as the Tao. By embracing the concepts of spontaneity, non-action, and harmony, Taoist philosophy teaches that one can wield influence without force or pressure. The Taoist approach to subtle influence entails monitoring and understanding the natural rhythms of a situation and then behaving in line with them, rather than trying to push one's will upon others.

Confucianism: The Art of Moral Influence
Confucianism places tremendous emphasis on moral character and virtuous behavior as the foundation of influence. According to Confucian principles, one can exert influence by embodying the virtues of compassion, righteousness, propriety, wisdom, and fidelity. By cultivating these values and leading by example, individuals can encourage others to follow their lead and gladly surrender to their

influence.

Buddhism: The Power of Compassion and Mindfulness

Buddhism teaches that true influence comes from a place of compassion and mindfulness. By gaining a deep understanding of the interconnectedness of all beings and exercising compassion towards others, one can produce a good ripple effect that inspires others around them. Mindfulness, the discipline of being fully present in the moment, allows individuals to observe and respond to situations with clarity and knowledge, enabling them to exert influence in a competent and compassionate manner.

The Synthesis of Eastern and Western Approaches

While Eastern philosophies offer unique insights into the art of subtle influence, they can be complemented by Western techniques to create a more comprehensive understanding. By incorporating the wisdom of both Eastern and Western philosophies, individuals can construct a nuanced and adaptive approach to influence that takes into consideration cultural differences and the difficulties of modern life.

In the next chapter, we will study the power dynamics that underlie subtle influence, analyzing the hierarchical structures, psychological elements, and perceptual biases that shape our interactions and impact the success of our influence techniques.

Eastern Philosophies' Subtle Power
In the quiet halls of old wisdom, Eastern philosophies have long held the secret to grasping the nuances of power, authority, and the delicate dance of influence. As we venture into the realms of shadows of authority, we must first understand the profound teachings that have formed the craft of subtle power throughout history.

The Tao of Influence is a central notion in Eastern philosophy, representing the natural order of things. Drawing on Taoism, we explore the essence of subtle power. The Tao teaches us the value of harmony and balance, as well as how to influence others without using force. Understanding the flow of the Tao becomes an essential tool for navigating the complicated webs of power in the shadows, where authority lives quietly.

Zen Buddhism emphasizes the skill of persuasion in its peaceful settings. It is not about loudly asserting power but rather about silently mastering comprehension. Meditation and mindfulness teach people how to communicate without using words, giving them an advantage in the subtle game of persuasion. In the shadows of authority, people who understand the power of quiet can wield the Zen approach with great skill.

Confucianism emphasizes ethics and moral leadership, offering a distinct viewpoint on authority. The subtle power comes from a leader's virtuous example, which inspires others to willingly follow suit. The concept of leading by moral influence rather than pure control resonates strongly in the halls of power, where the shadows cast by a virtuous leader can mold the fate of nations.

Martial arts, steeped in Eastern traditions, entail more than only physical battle but also strategic diplomacy. Sun Tzu's art of war demonstrates the need for strategic subtlety. In the Shadows of Authority, mastering the martial art of diplomacy becomes critical as nations engage in a delicate balance of power in which strength lies not just in military might but also in clever political maneuvering.

Political intrigue resonates with the concept of yin and yang, which represents the duality of reality. The shadows of authority thrive in the delicate balance of competing powers. Understanding the cyclical nature of power, in which rise and fall are unavoidable, gives a road map for anyone attempting to navigate the subtle currents that form personal and political destiny.

As we peel back the layers of Eastern philosophy's subtle potency, we find ourselves at the crossroads of history and intrigue. The Shadows of Authority, with their cryptic attraction, invite us to investigate the ancient wisdom that has fashioned the art of influence and the fates of individuals and nations alike.

This research reveals the eternal secrets that lead us through the complex dance of power dynamics.

The   Influence   Tao
The idea of the Tao, a basic idea that includes the universe's inherent order, is at the core of Eastern philosophies. The Tao instructs us to follow the cycles of life and to accept its flow. When it comes to influence, the Tao advises people to watch and adjust to the dynamics of their surroundings rather than forcing their will on   them.

The Taoist perspective on influence places a strong emphasis on fostering inner peace and avoiding pointless strife. One can use influence without using force or manipulation by putting themselves in line with the natural order of things. This way of thinking instructs us to watch, have patience, and act appropriately when the time is right.

The   Presence   Zen
Zen Buddhism provides important insights into the art of subtle influence because of its emphasis on attention and presence. Zen encourages us to listen intently, to be totally present in each moment, and to observe without passing judgment. We may tune into the finer points of human connection and

react with compassion and clarity by practicing heightened awareness.

In the sphere of influence, the Zen approach advises us to put others' needs and desires ahead of our own ego-driven ones. Active listening and sympathetic understanding are two skills that help us connect with people more deeply and gain their trust. The Zen school of thought serves as a reminder that sincere concern for others and authenticity are the foundations of true influence.

The Virtuous Confucian Path
With its focus on moral principles and social peace, Confucianism offers a framework for comprehending the ethical aspects of influence. According to Confucius, power should be used wisely, kindly, and in accordance with the precepts of virtue. The Confucian way of life exhorts people to develop their moral fiber, set an example for others, and motivate others by their deeds.

The Confucian perspective on influence places a strong emphasis on developing harmonious relationships and a foundation of trust. Having honesty, compassion, and humility in one's life will win one the respect and admiration of others. Confucianism serves as a helpful reminder that genuine influence comes from motivating people to become their best selves rather than from using force to control them.

The Influence Yin and Yang
With its origins in ancient Chinese philosophy, the idea of Yin and Yang provides important insights into the mechanics of influence. Yang stands for the energetic, aggressive, and direct components of influence, whereas Yin represents the receptive, intuitive, and subtle qualities. In the art of influence, harmony and balance are achieved by the interaction of Yin and Yang.

We can handle the complexity of power dynamics with grace and delicacy when we grasp the Yin and Yang of influence. It teaches us to know when to talk and when to listen, when to make an assertive move and when to give up. Accepting the Yin and Yang of influence allows us to modify our tactics for various circumstances and develop a more comprehensive method of exercising power.

To sum up, the Eastern philosophies provide valuable perspectives on the skill of subtle persuasion. The Confucian way emphasizes the value of virtue and harmonious relationships, the Tao teaches us to align ourselves with the natural order, the Zen philosophy calls us to be fully present and compassionate, and the idea of Yin and Yang serves as a reminder of the need for balance and adaptability. We can negotiate the intricacies of power dynamics with discernment, moral rectitude, and grace by incorporating these lessons into our comprehension of influence.

The Dance of Shadows

2.1 Authority and Hierarchy

Within the complex network of power relations, hierarchy and authority are essential in determining the sphere of influence. Anyone hoping to become an expert in subtle influence must comprehend the dynamics and structure of these components. We shall explore the depths of authority and hierarchy in this chapter, revealing the unseen forces that control power dynamics.

2.1.1 The Hierarchical Foundations

A basic feature of human civilizations that has existed in many ways throughout history is hierarchy. It's a method of putting people or groups in a structured hierarchy according to their perceived authority, power, or position. Hierarchies have influenced and molded social interactions and power dynamics throughout history, from ancient societies to contemporary organizations.

Fundamentally, hierarchy creates a distinct chain of command, with various people holding varying degrees of power. By offering a framework for decision-making, resource allocation, and power distribution, this vertical organization fosters stability and order. In any given institution, be it a monarchy, a business, or a social group, hierarchies establish the duties and responsibilities of each member.

2.1.2 The Authority Dynamics

Authority is the capacity or right to issue commands, render judgments, and impose compliance. It is intimately related to hierarchy. Because it gives people the power to influence and control others, it is the main factor that keeps hierarchies working. Formal authority can come from personal traits or experience, or it can be informal and come from positions of leadership or management.

Authority relationships are intricate and multidimensional. A person can acquire authority from a variety of factors, such as experience, standing, reputation, or charisma. It can be regarded as genuine if it is founded on official duties and positions, or it can be perceived if others acknowledge and accept a person's influence. Navigating the complexities of power dynamics requires an understanding of the sources and dynamics of authority.

2.1.3 Exposing the Framework Authority and hierarchies are dynamic systems that change and adapt over time rather than being static things. Understanding the hierarchy's structure, the main actors, and the power dynamics at work are necessary before attempting to navigate the dance of power. This calls for close attention to detail, attentive listening, and a thorough comprehension of the organizational and social context.

Understanding the formal and informal power patterns within a hierarchy can help one better understand how authority is distributed and how people relate to one another. A strategic approach to subtle influence is made possible by identifying the sources of authority and the places of influence. This enables people to use their comprehension of power dynamics to further their objectives.

2.1.4 Authority and Hierarchies' Effects Human interactions and conduct are significantly influenced by authority and hierarchy. They affect people's attitudes, motives, and behaviors by forming their perceptions of themselves and other people. People in positions of leadership frequently have a lot of power, which can be used for good or bad, depending on the situation.

In order to influence others in an ethical and successful way, one must comprehend the effects of hierarchy and authority. It calls for a careful balancing act between asserting one's own authority and deferring to that of others. People can dance the influence dance with integrity, making sure that their actions are consistent with their principles and advance the common good, by acknowledging the underlying power dynamics at work.

The psychology of influence will be examined in the following section, where we will delve into the complex mechanisms of the human psyche and the elements that determine how we perceive and react to authority. People who comprehend the psychological foundations of influence can create tactics to move deftly and skillfully through the power dance.

2.2 The Influence Psychology

Knowing the psychology of influence is crucial in the complex dance of power relations. One must delve into the depths of human behavior, motivations, and perceptions in order to master the art of subtle influence. This chapter delves into the psychological principles that determine the dynamics of influence, offering priceless insights into the art of persuasion and throwing light on the complex inner workings of the human mind.

2.2.1 Persuasion's Power

Persuasion is the fundamental tool of influence. The skill of persuasion involves persuading people to embrace a specific viewpoint, mindset, or way of acting. The influencer tries to mold the ideas and behavior of others in a delicate dance between the influenced and the influencer. Anyone hoping to use influence effectively must comprehend the psychological concepts underlying persuasion.

The elaboration likelihood model is a highly important theory of persuasion (ELM). This approach proposes that people process persuasive messages in two different ways: centrally and peripherally. The fundamental approach entails a methodical and deliberate analysis of the content, based on reason, logic, and evidence. Conversely, the peripheral path depends on indicators like physical appeal, trustworthiness, and emotional attractions.

Knowing which path people are most likely to choose allows an influencer to adjust their message appropriately. For instance, it would be more successful to give logical arguments and supporting data if the audience is inclined to use the central route processing technique. Stressing the influencer's legitimacy and beauty, on the other hand, might be more effective if the audience is more inclined to depend on ancillary clues.

2.2.2 Cognitive Biases' Function
Human decision-making is greatly influenced by cognitive biases, which can also be used to covertly affect others. These biases are systematic mistakes in reasoning that cause people to stray from making logical decisions. Through comprehension and application of these prejudices, an influencer can mold opinions and direct choices.

Confirmation bias is one such prejudice that causes people to ignore evidence that contradicts their preexisting ideas in favor of information that supports those beliefs. An influencer can alter opinions and reinforce preexisting beliefs by delivering information selectively that supports the desired goal.

The halo effect, which happens when people attach positive traits or characteristics to someone based on a single positive trait or characteristic, is another potent cognitive bias. An influencer might take advantage of the halo effect to build credibility and influence by projecting a favorable image and emphasizing one particular desired trait.

2.2.3 The Significance of Social Proof Because we are social beings, humans frequently turn to other people for advice on how to feel, think, and act. Social proof is a phenomenon that has the potential to be a powerful instrument for influence. People are more inclined to follow the example of others when they are unsure about how to proceed.

With the growth of social media and online communities in the digital era, social proof has assumed new forms. Large-following influencers have the power to sway public opinion, fashion, and purchasing habits. Influencers can establish a consensus and persuade others to embrace their viewpoints or actions by utilizing the social proof effect.

2.2.4 The Function of Feelings

Emotions may be a potent influencer and play a significant part in decision-making. Messages that are emotionally charged have a greater ability to grab attention, provoke a reaction, and influence behavior. An influencer can connect with others and inspire action by appealing to their emotions.

Empathy and compassion are two powerful emotions to draw upon. An influencer can elicit empathy and motivate action by drawing attention to the suffering of others or making an appeal to shared values. Moreover, one can utilize optimistic feelings like happiness, excitement, and optimism to energize and inspire others.

2.2.5 Framing's Power

Information perception and interpretation can be greatly influenced by the manner in which it is presented. When information is presented in a way that influences people's understanding and assessment of it, it's referred to as framing. An influencer can sway opinions and direct choices by presenting facts in a positive manner.

One way to make a message more enticing is to frame it in terms of possible advantages rather than drawbacks. Similar to this, presenting a topic as one of individual liberty as opposed to governmental regulation may cause distinct reactions. An influencer can sway the story and affect the result by carefully choosing the framing.

Gaining proficiency in the art of subtle influence requires an understanding of influence psychology. Through skillful use of persuasion, cognitive biases, social proof, emotions, and framing, an influencer can deftly negotiate the complex dance of power relations. But it's important to approach influence in an ethical and responsible manner, taking responsibility for one's actions and weighing one's own interests against the greater good.

2.3 Perception's Function in Subtle Effect

Perception has a crucial role in the complex dance of subtle impact. The effectiveness of our influence can be significantly impacted by how we and others view each other. We may move with grace and accuracy through the complex web of human interaction when we are aware of the power of perception. In this chapter, we will examine the different aspects of perception and how they relate to the subtle influence of art.

2.3.1 The Influence of Initial Views

According to a proverb, "You never get a second chance to make a first impression." This also applies to the domain of subtle influence. The first impression that people have of us determines the dynamics of the relationship as a whole. The way we show up in those vital initial moments can influence how others view our integrity and intentions, whether in a personal or professional context.

It is crucial to pay attention to our appearance, body language, and vocal communication in order to create a good first impression. Posing properly, speaking with confidence, and dressing correctly for the situation can all help create a positive impression. Furthermore, building rapport and trust early on in interactions can be facilitated by paying attention and showing real interest in others.

2.3.2 The Significance of Nonverbal Expression

Words are important, but nonverbal clues frequently convey more information than spoken words. Our tone of speech, facial expressions, and body language can all give off subliminal cues that affect how other people see us. Mastering the art of subtle influence requires an understanding of and the ability to use nonverbal communication.

A sense of connection and trust can be established by keeping eye contact, projecting an open and carefree body language, and imitating the expressions and actions of others. On the other hand, defensiveness or indifference can be shown by crossed arms, fidgeting, or averting eye contact, which may make it more difficult for us to persuade people.

Nonverbal cues can change throughout cultures, so it's critical to recognize these variations and modify our nonverbal communication accordingly. Our nonverbal cues can help us build a sense of familiarity and understanding with the people we are trying to influence by matching theirs.

2.3.3 Perceived Expertise's Power

One important factor in the art of subtle influence is perceived expertise. People are more inclined to respect and believe what we have to say when they think we are informed and skilled in a given field. Gaining proficiency in a certain area can improve our capacity to gently sway other people.

It is critical that we keep learning new things and developing our abilities in the field of our choice in order to build perceived expertise. This can be accomplished by continuing our education, keeping abreast of business developments, and aggressively looking for chances to demonstrate our skills. By providing insightful commentary and addressing problems, we may enhance our standing as authorities.

But it's crucial to find a middle ground between showcasing your knowledge and coming across as haughty or patronizing. Our reputation may be strengthened, and cooperative relationships can be fostered by humility and a willingness to learn from others, which will ultimately increase our influence.

2.3.4 Emotional Intelligence's Power

A key component of perception under subtle influence is emotional intelligence, or the capacity to identify and comprehend emotions in oneself and others. Understanding the emotions of people around us allows us to modify our strategy and communication style to better meet their needs and preferences.

Empathy, a crucial aspect of emotional intelligence, enables us to establish more meaningful connections with people. We may establish rapport and trust with them by truly understanding and validating their feelings, which will facilitate our ability to sway their opinions and choices.

Emotional intelligence also helps us control our own feelings, which helps us avoid rash decisions that could damage our authority. We can project stability and control, which increases our perceived influence, by being collected and calm under pressure.

2.3.5 Perception Management's Power

In the art of subtle persuasion, controlling our perceptions of others is a calculated risk. In order to achieve our targeted results, perception management entails meticulously sculpting and selecting our image. We may sway how people see us and the circumstances we find ourselves in by crafting the story around our deeds and intentions.

Self-awareness and a knowledge of how others interpret our words and actions are necessary for perception control. We can cultivate a reputation that supports our intended influence by constantly acting with honesty, sincerity, and consistency.

It's crucial to remember, though, that manipulation or dishonesty are not the same as perception management. Our actions should constantly be guided by ethical concerns to make sure that our influence is founded on sincerity and good intentions.

In summary, perception is essential to the skill of subtle persuasion. We can dance the complex dance of influence with skill and efficacy if we understand and use the power of first impressions, nonverbal communication, perceived competence, emotional intelligence, and perception management. By becoming adept at perceiving people, we can mold their opinion of ourselves and therefore impact their attitudes, choices, and behaviors.

2.4 Tidying Up the Power Structure

The talent that distinguishes the expert influencer from the ordinary player in the complex dance of power dynamics is the capacity to control the balance of power. Reaching your objectives and influencing people may depend on your ability to skillfully tip the odds in your favor. This chapter delves into the skill of balancing power, looking at the methods and approaches used by historical leaders who have perfected this difficult dance.

2.4.1 Taking Advantage of Flaws and Vulnerabilities

Exploiting flaws and vulnerabilities is one of the best strategies to shift the balance of power. You can strategically take advantage of the flaws of people in positions of power or influence by figuring out how they work. This could include revealing private information, taking advantage of fears, or profiting from prior errors. However, as taking advantage of weaknesses can have dire repercussions and even irreversibly harm relationships, it is crucial to use caution and ethical considerations when using this method.

2.4.2 Forming Coalitions and Alliances

The formation of coalitions and alliances is a

potent tactic for shifting the balance of power. You can increase your influence and put pressure on those in positions of power by building strategic alliances with others who have similar objectives or interests. Throughout history, social activists, corporate moguls, and political figures have all used this strategy. However, as it can be difficult to preserve the delicate balance of power within a coalition, forging alliances takes rigorous discussion, compromise, and trust-building.

2.4.3 Regulating Perception and Information

In the era of information, narrative management and public perception manipulation are powerful tools for shifting the power dynamic. You may shape how other people see you and your rivals by selectively distributing information and deftly arranging how it is presented. This can entail using the power of framing, constructing compelling messages, and selectively exposing or concealing facts. However, as falsifying information can have serious repercussions and damage credibility, it is imperative that we use this strategy with ethics and responsibility.

2.4.4 Making the Most of Assets and Resources

Using assets and resources strategically is

another powerful way to bend the odds in your favor. Gaining a substantial edge over others can be achieved by recognizing and utilizing the resources at your disposal, such as financial capital, intellectual property, or powerful contacts. This strategy calls for strategic planning, savvy resource management, and the capacity to recognize opportunities where your resources can have the most possible impact. However, it is crucial to exercise this authority sensibly and morally because misusing resources without taking the larger good into account might have unfavorable effects.

2.4.5 Adjusting to Shifting Conditions The skill of navigating changing dynamics and being adaptive is also necessary for altering the balance of power. Power systems are dynamic, and retaining influence requires the capacity to identify and adjust to shifting conditions. This could entail changing tactics, creating new coalitions, or reassessing how resources are allocated. Being aware of how power relations are constantly changing will help you strategically position yourself and maintain your influence even in the face of uncertainty.

2.4.6 Moral Points to Remember

Even though it can be a powerful tool, the art of shifting the balance of power requires careful consideration of the moral consequences of your actions. The quest for influence shouldn't compromise moral values or come at the expense of other people's well-being. Finding a balance between reaching your objectives and behaving honorably is crucial. You may make sure that your influence is used sensibly and for the benefit of society at large by abiding by ethical standards.

The art of observation will be covered in detail in the following chapter, along with the benefits of active listening, how to read nonverbal clues, and how to uncover hidden intentions and motivations. You can improve your capacity to alter the balance of power and obtain important insights into the dynamics of power by developing your observational abilities.

Mastering the Art of Observation

3.1 The Influence of Paying Attention

The ability to actively listen is one of our most powerful instruments in the complex dance of subtle influence. The act of genuinely understanding and listening to people can have a significant impact on our capacity for persuasion and influence, despite its seemingly straightforward nature. By developing this ability, we can make stronger relationships with people around us, understand unsaid messages, and unearth hidden motives.

3.1.1 The Presence Art

Being completely present in the moment and offering the speaker our whole attention are key components of active listening, which goes beyond just hearing what is being said. Putting aside our own biases, assumptions, and distractions is necessary to create an environment where the speaker feels appreciated and heard. By doing this, we establish a setting that encourages direct and honest conversation and provides the groundwork for effective influence.

3.1.2 Compassion and Perception

We must practice empathy and make an effort to comprehend the speaker's point of view if we are to listen well. This entails empathizing with someone, holding off on passing judgment, and accepting their feelings and experiences. We may build rapport and trust with people by empathizing with them, which increases the likelihood that they will be open to our thoughts and proposals.

3.1.3 Initiating Involvement

Engaging in active engagement with the speaker is a component of active listening, which surpasses passive receiving. Nonverbal clues like keeping eye contact, nodding in agreement, and employing the right facial expressions can be used to illustrate this. Furthermore, confirming that we have accurately comprehended the speaker's message by asking clarifying questions and paraphrasing what they have said demonstrates real interest.

3.1.4 Discovering Latent Connotations

The real message is frequently hidden in the subtleties of language and nonverbal clues, lying just beneath the surface. We are able to discern these nuances and unearth hidden meanings when we actively listen. We can learn about the speaker's feelings, goals, and underlying motivations by observing their tone of voice, body language, and facial expressions. We may more effectively shape our responses and affect their perceptions thanks to this improved understanding.

3.1.5 Establishing Relationships and Trust

Establishing connection and trust with others can be facilitated by using active listening techniques. Sincere listening makes the other person feel important and understood, which promotes mutual respect and trust. Since a solid relationship is built on trust, there is a greater chance that our influence will be welcomed and acknowledged. We establish a long-lasting foundation of trust by exhibiting our dedication to comprehending and assisting people.

3.1.6 Getting Past Obstacles to Active Listening

Although it's a useful talent, active listening is not without its difficulties. Distractions abound in our fast-paced environment, making it challenging to offer others our full attention. Furthermore, our capacity to listen and comprehend with genuineness can be impeded by our own prejudices and assumptions. It will take deliberate effort and a dedication to being totally present in our interactions for us to overcome these obstacles. We may improve our active listening abilities and increase our effectiveness as influencers by identifying and resolving these challenges.

3.1.7 The Influence of Quiet

One powerful instrument in the practice of active listening is silence. Silence for a short while gives the speaker room to think and communicate more fully. Additionally, silence allows us to gather information and consider our responses. Respecting the speaker's words by remaining silent inspires them to continue expressing their ideas and emotions.

3.1.8 Using Active Listening in Daily Situations

Active listening is a talent that can be used in any situation and is not just appropriate for formal situations. Active listening enables us to build closer bonds, settle disputes, and have a beneficial impact on people in social, professional, and personal contexts. We can gracefully and deftly negotiate the complexity of interpersonal connections by deliberately trying to listen intently.

Active listening is a fundamental ability in the dance of subtle influence that facilitates impactful communication. Through the practice of presence, empathy, and active participation, we can develop stronger relationships, unearth hidden meanings, and establish trust with those around us. We can gracefully and skillfully negotiate the shadows of authority by using the power of active listening, making sure that we never overshadow others in positions of authority.

3.2   Interpreting   Silence

Words are not always the best gauge of genuine intentions in the complex dance of subtle influence. The most insightful revelations are frequently found in the unstated, unsaid, and nonverbal clues that permeate our relationships. Learning to read between the lines and interpret the subliminal messages is essential to becoming a true observational expert. The power of reading nonverbal signs, comprehending motives and covert objectives, spotting patterns, forecasting behavior, and the skill of information collection will all be covered in this chapter.

3.2.1   Interpreting   Nonverbal   Signs

The process of communication is complex and involves much more than just spoken words. Body language, tone of voice, and facial expressions are examples of nonverbal clues that frequently carry more meaning than words alone. You can learn a lot about a person's genuine feelings and thoughts by developing your ability to read these subtle cues.

For instance, facial expressions can convey a lot of information. A wrinkled brow might convey uncertainty or worry, while a raised eyebrow can convey surprise or suspicion. In the same vein, a smile might be forced or sincere, expressing warmth or a secret purpose. You can learn more about someone's intentions and decipher hidden meanings by closely observing these nonverbal indicators.

Another effective method for reading concealed signals is body language. Body language, gestures, and physical closeness can all give away information about how at ease, confident, and involved someone is. For example, open and relaxed body language may represent receptiveness and trust, but crossed arms may signal defensiveness or opposition. You can modify your approach and craft your message to more effectively connect with the other person by paying attention to these nonverbal indications.

Another important component of nonverbal communication is the tone of voice. Pitch, loudness, and rhythm of speech can all give away an individual's emotional state and hidden agenda. Whereas a hasty or forceful tone may imply impatience or ulterior goals, a calm and measured tone may reflect sincerity. You can learn more about the speaker's genuine intentions by paying close attention to these minute details.

3.2.2 Recognizing Hidden Agendas and Motivations

In the world of subtle influence, it is critical to comprehend the intentions and hidden motives of people. Individuals are motivated by a complicated web of fears, ambitions, and goals; by understanding these underlying reasons, you can better predict their behavior and adjust your strategy accordingly.

Asking insightful questions and practicing active listening are crucial for revealing hidden motives. You may establish a secure environment for others to express their thoughts and emotions by really demonstrating attention and understanding. By closely examining their words, tone, and body language, you can spot trends or contradictions that could indicate what their genuine objectives are.

It's also critical to take into account the larger context of the encounters. External influences, including cultural norms, personal experiences, and social conventions, frequently mold people's motivations. You can better comprehend the underlying dynamics that shape human behavior by being aware of these environmental influences.

3.2.3 Examining Trends and Forecasting Action

The threads that bind together human activity are called patterns. You can learn a great deal about other people's motivations and behaviors by examining these trends. Pattern analysis is a key skill in the art of subtle influence, whether it is used to spot trends, detect recurrent habits, or forecast future behavior.

Using data to examine trends is one efficient method. You can find trends and correlations that might not be immediately obvious by gathering and examining pertinent data. With the abundance of readily available data in the digital era, this can be especially helpful. Making better decisions and revealing hidden patterns can be achieved by utilizing data analysis.

Using psychological profiling is another method for examining patterns. You can learn a lot about people's likely behaviors and responses by researching their values, beliefs, and personality traits. This can be especially helpful in scenarios where you have to predict other people's behavior and adjust your strategy accordingly.

3.2.4 The Skill of Information Gathering Knowledge is power in the dance of subtle influence. For the purpose of comprehending the dynamics of a situation and developing workable tactics, the capacity to obtain and evaluate information is essential. But it's crucial to handle information collection in an ethical and responsible manner, keeping confidentiality and privacy limits in mind.

Using open-ended questions and active listening are two efficient methods of information gathering. You can inspire others to offer insightful opinions and viewpoints by holding meaningful conversations and posing intelligent questions. By doing this, you can establish rapport and trust with the people you engage with, in addition to helping you obtain information.

Research and observation are two other methods of obtaining information. You may learn a lot about people's intentions and motives by paying close attention to their acts and behaviors. Furthermore, learning more about pertinent subjects and doing research might give you a deeper comprehension of the environment in which you work.

It is crucial to remember that information collection should always be carried out morally and legally. Maintaining privacy, getting permission when needed, and responsible information use are fundamental values in the search for knowledge.

3.2.5   The   Observational   Ethics

Even though the skill of observation is a useful instrument in the field of subtle influence, we must always think about the moral consequences of our actions. It can be difficult to draw clear lines between privacy invasion and observation, so it's critical to walk this fine line with honesty and consideration for others.

Recognizing and upholding the boundaries that people have set for themselves is a necessary part of respecting privacy. It entails not intruding on private affairs or utilizing knowledge gleaned from observation in an unfavorable or manipulative way. In order to respect privacy, we must also ask for permission when appropriate and be open and honest about the goals and parameters of our observations.

It's also critical to think about the possible ramifications of our findings. Will others be harmed or distressed by our actions? Will they undermine relationships or undermine trust? As we work through the ethical challenges of observation, these are crucial questions for us to ask ourselves.

In summary, the ability to see past surface-level cues is crucial to mastering the art of subliminal persuasion. Through the deciphering of nonverbal clues, comprehension of goals and concealed agendas, examination of patterns, and ethical collection of information, we can acquire a significant understanding of the dynamics of human interaction. But it's crucial to approach these behaviors with moral rectitude and consideration for other people, understanding the moral bounds that guide our behavior.

3.3 Recognizing Motives and Covert Plans

Gaining insight into the intentions and covert plans of others in our immediate vicinity is an essential ability in the complex dance of subtle influence. A master of subtle influence must be able to read people's underlying intentions and aspirations, just as a talented dancer reads their partner's motions. We can better comprehend and skillfully traverse the complex web of power dynamics by looking into the shadows of human motivation.

3.3.1 The Intricacy of Incentives

Human conduct is driven by the complex idea of motivation. It is the unseen force that motivates people to take specific actions, frequently driven by their needs, wants, and ambitions. Thoughts are not always clear-cut, and people sometimes harbor ulterior motives that they are reluctant to discuss in public. Uncovering these covert motives and comprehending the intricate relationship between conscious and unconscious wants are essential skills for anyone hoping to become a subtle influence expert.

3.3.2 Exposing Covert Motives

Individuals may have covert goals that are not

immediately visible to others, which are known as hidden agendas. These agendas, which can range from political ploys to personal aspirations, frequently influence the choices and behaviors of individuals in positions of authority. Learning to read between the lines and recognize the tiny clues that reveal people's genuine intentions is essential to uncovering hidden agendas.

3.3.3 The Observational Power
The secret to deciphering concealed goals and motivations is observation. Through close observation of people's words, behaviors, and nonverbal signs, we can learn a great deal about their genuine intentions. By employing the skill of active listening, which entails hearing what the speaker is saying as well as understanding and sympathizing with them, we can ascertain the true intentions behind their statements. Through the use of body language, tone of voice, and facial expressions, we can pick up on tiny cues that point to ulterior motives.

3.3.4 Recognizing Trends and Forecasting Behavior
Behavior patterns can offer important hints about the intentions and motives of an individual. We can learn more about

someone's fundamental goals and intentions by examining their previous choices and actions to find reoccurring patterns. With this knowledge, we may forecast future actions and speculate about people's possible reactions to certain circumstances. We can strategically position ourselves to influence results in our favor by remaining one step ahead of the game.

3.3.5 Information Gathering as an Art

Getting information from a variety of sources is crucial to revealing motives and covert plans. This can entail gathering information through study, having discussions, and forming bonds with people who might know something about the motivations of those we want to sway. We can assemble a more thorough picture of the driving forces and covert objectives at work by gathering and examining data.

3.3.6 The Observational Ethics

Even though deciphering motives and covert goals is a valuable skill, we must always think about the moral ramifications of the things we do. We should always act with dignity and respect for other people's privacy. In order to ensure that our quest for knowledge does not violate the rights or welfare of others, it is imperative that we find a balance between the acquisition of information and respecting boundaries.

Knowing motives and hidden intentions is a talent that can improve one's ability to navigate power relations in the complex dance of subtle influence. Examining the dark side of human drive helps us comprehend the intricate relationship between conscious and unconscious wants. Equipped with this understanding, we can place ourselves in a way that will strategically affect results while upholding our sense of moral obligation. The skill of deciphering motives and covert objectives demands a fine balance between perceptive observation and a deep comprehension of the moral ramifications of our choices. In Chapter 4, we will examine the craft of strategic communication and the potency of framing as we delve deeper into the shadows of influence.

3.4 Examining Trends and Forecasting Action

An essential skill in the complex dance of subtle influence is the capacity to recognize trends and forecast behavior. One can anticipate people's actions and adjust their own plans by knowing their underlying motivations and hidden agendas. In order to give readers the skills they need to skillfully and precisely negotiate the intricate web of human interactions, this chapter examines the art of identifying patterns and forecasting the future.

3.4.1 The Observational Power
The art of identifying patterns and forecasting behavior is based primarily on observation. One can learn a great deal about the thoughts, feelings, and intentions of people by closely monitoring their behaviors, words, and nonverbal signs. This calls for a sharpened awareness and a readiness to look below the obvious and beyond what is said outright.

3.4.2 Interpreting Nonverbal Signs
A person's genuine intentions are frequently more apparent through nonverbal indicators than through words. A person's emotional

state and underlying motivations can be inferred from their tone of voice, body language, and facial expressions. Gaining proficiency in reading between the lines allows one to see hidden meanings and predict future behaviors.

3.4.3 Identifying Trends
The threads that bind seemingly unconnected behaviors and occurrences together are called patterns. People can be better understood as individuals, and their future behavior can be predicted by identifying recurrent patterns in their behavior. This calls for exacting attention to detail as well as the capacity to recognize minute variations and similarities.

3.4.4 Examining Incentives
Predicting people's behavior requires an understanding of their underlying motivations. Humans are frequently led by a complex web of anxieties, ambitions, and goals. One can predict their activities and adjust their own strategy to effectively influence people by examining their fundamental reasons.

3.4.5 Behavior Prediction
Behavior prediction is both a science and an art. It necessitates a thorough comprehension

of human psychology, the capacity for knowledge synthesis, and a readiness to follow one's gut. Making educated guesses about future behavior is possible by integrating knowledge from observation, interpreting nonverbal signs, identifying trends, and examining motivations.

3.4.6 The Significance of Context

When examining patterns and forecasting behavior, context is crucial. Social dynamics, personal circumstances, and the environment all have an impact on people's behavior. One can better comprehend people's behavior and make more accurate forecasts by taking into account the larger context in which they operate.

3.4.7 Information Gathering

Relevant data must be gathered in order to examine patterns and forecast behavior. This entails proactively pursuing knowledge via discussions, investigation, and scrutiny. More accurate forecasts can be made by painting a more complete picture of people and their motivations through the collection of thorough data.

3.4.8 The Adaptability Art

Although the ability to see trends and forecast

behavior is useful, it's crucial to maintain flexibility in one's strategy. People are complicated, and even the sharpest observer can be taken aback. One can modify plans and forecasts as conditions change by remaining flexible and receptive to new information.

3.4.9 Moral Points to Remember
Analyzing patterns and forecasting behavior requires careful consideration of ethical issues, as with any aspect of subtle influence. It is crucial to apply this information honorably and ethically. Rather than being used to control or take advantage of other people, the capacity to foresee behavior could be utilized to promote favorable results and create deep connections.

3.4.10: The Influence Dance
Predicting behavior and analyzing patterns is a dance of influence in and of itself. It calls for a careful balancing act between intuition, strategic thinking, and observation. Gaining mastery of this skill will enable one to gracefully and deftly negotiate the complexities of interpersonal interactions, using their comprehension of others to further their objectives while upholding moral principles.

The art of information gathering will be discussed in the next part, along with the several methods and approaches that can be used to gain the understanding required for accurate analysis and prediction.

3.5 The Skill of Information Gathering

Knowledge is power in the complex dance of subtle influence. Gaining insight into the intentions and hidden motives of people around you is an essential skill that can significantly improve your capacity to negotiate power relations. We will examine information collection in this chapter, giving you the skills and methods to become a skilled observer and source of insightful information.

3.5.1 Observational Power

The skill of obtaining knowledge is based primarily on observation. The skill of observing subtleties in communication, whether expressed orally or nonverbally, can disclose a great deal about someone's intentions, feelings, and ideas. You can find hidden facts and comprehend the dynamics at work better by developing your observational abilities.

Active listening is one of the most effective techniques in the art of observation. You can discern subtle clues and nuances that may disclose someone's genuine intentions if you pay close attention to what they have to say. Be mindful of their tone of voice, facial expressions, and body language in addition to the words they say. These can offer insightful information about their intentions and emotional state.

3.5.2 Interpreting Nonverbal Signs

Words are frequently not as powerful as nonverbal clues. Gaining the ability to interpret these signs and read between the lines might offer you a big advantage when it comes to acquiring information. For instance, a person's body language might convey their degree of ease or discomfort, confidence or insecurity, and even interest or disinterest in a certain subject or circumstance.

Another effective way to convey nonverbal cues is through facial expressions. Particularly telling are microexpressions—brief facial expressions that convey genuine emotions. Even when someone is attempting to hide their genuine emotions, you can still learn a lot about them by being able to identify and decipher these subtle signs of emotion.

Nonverbal signs such as posture, eye contact, and gestures should also be taken into account. A person's posture might convey their degree of confidence or surrender, while their gestures can convey their level of involvement or anger. Making or not making eye contact might provide information about someone's honesty and reliability.

3.5.3 Recognizing Hidden Agendas and Motivations

Knowing the intentions and covert plans of people you are watching is crucial to efficiently gathering information. Individuals are motivated by a multitude of things, such as anxieties, insecurities, aspirations, and personal goals. Gaining insight into these fundamental drives can help you predict their behavior and adjust your strategy accordingly.

Asking pointed questions and having thoughtful conversations are two ways to find reasons. Open-ended inquiries allow you to learn more about someone's values, objectives, and priorities while also paying attention to their answers. Additionally, you may learn a lot about someone's interests and worries by observing the subjects they choose to address or avoid.

It's also critical to be mindful of the possibility of ulterior motives. Individuals could not be open about their true intentions or hidden agendas. You can begin to identify these hidden objectives by noticing any patterns of conduct, as well as discrepancies in their words and behaviors. But it's important to proceed cautiously and refrain from drawing conclusions too quickly without enough data.

3.5.4 Recognizing Trends and Forecasting Behavior

Behavior patterns can provide important details about the objectives and character of an individual. You can start making predictions about people's likely behavior in various scenarios by keeping an eye on and examining these trends. This capacity for prediction can be a useful tool for learning and affecting results.

Observe whether there are any patterns or habits in the way that person behaves. When presented with a specific opportunity or problem, do they regularly behave in a certain way? Do they follow any patterns when making decisions? You can learn more about their motivations and mental processes by recognizing these tendencies.

It is crucial to remember that although patterns might provide useful information, they are not always reliable predictors of future behavior. Humans are complex beings who occasionally shock us with their behavior. As such, it's critical to maintain objectivity in your observations and modify your tactics as necessary.

3.5.5 The Observational Ethics

Even if information collection is an art, it's important to think about the ethical ramifications of your conduct. Your quest of knowledge should always be guided by respect for one's personal space and limits. It's critical to collect data in an ethical and responsible manner, respecting the rights and dignity of others at all times.

Respecting boundaries entails staying away from deceit and manipulation and gathering knowledge through legal channels. It also entails being aware of the possible fallout from your choices. Think about how your observations might affect other people and whether the advantages outweigh the disadvantages.

Furthermore, it's critical to make responsible use of the data you collect. The application of knowledge should be done so with caution and regard for other people's welfare. Refrain from utilizing information to take advantage of or manipulate people for your own gain. Rather, make an effort to apply your knowledge to promote empathy, cultivate connections, and effect constructive change.

Gaining proficiency in information collecting will help you become more adept at negotiating power relationships and influencing people subtly. Always remember to approach this skill with honor and integrity, and instead of manipulating or controlling others, use your knowledge to empower yourself and others. Through consistent practice and a dedication to moral behavior, you can develop into an expert observer and source of insightful information.

3.6   Observational   Ethics

When it comes to the art of subtle influence, observation is a valuable weapon. By paying close attention to other people, we can learn a great deal about their intentions, behaviors, and motives. With this understanding, we may adjust our strategy and messaging to successfully influence and persuade. To make sure that we don't cross lines or use others as leverage for our own gain, we must carefully analyze the ethics of observation.

3.6.1 Honoring Consent and Privacy

Respecting individuals' privacy and consent is essential when making observations. It is not only unethical but frequently unlawful to violate someone else's private or personal space without that person's knowledge or consent. Setting up boundaries and getting permission are crucial while doing any kind of observation, particularly in private.

Respecting the company's privacy and observation policies and guidelines is crucial in professional settings. Be mindful of the limits that your company has established, and make sure that everything you do complies with moral principles. When observing or obtaining information about others, always get permission beforehand, especially in delicate circumstances.

3.6.2 Juggling Individual Rights with the Greater Good

While observation can yield insightful information, it is crucial to maintain a balance between the rights of the individual and the greater good. Respect, independence, and well-being should never be sacrificed in the name of power. It is essential to think about the possible repercussions of our choices and make sure that our observations don't hurt or take advantage of other people.

Consider if your aims are in line with moral standards while you watch other people. Are you utilizing observation to manipulate or control, or are you trying to comprehend and empathize? Make an effort to apply what you see to further constructive goals like cooperation, relationship-building, and understanding.

3.6.3 Honesty and Transparency

Upholding integrity and openness in our observations is essential to moral behavior. It is crucial to be clear about our aims and the reason for our actions, whether we are monitoring people or acquiring information. Being open and honest fosters trust and enables others to choose their involvement with knowledge.

Make sure you get participants' informed consent and are explicit about the goal of the study when you conduct research or collect data. When disclosing results, respect their right to withdraw at any moment and maintain their privacy and anonymity.

3.6.4 Steer clear of exploitation and manipulation.

Never use observation to control or take advantage of other people. Understanding the power dynamics at work is essential, as is making sure that our observations don't worsen the situation for others or add to the power disparity. Refrain from exploiting personal information about people that you have observed to exert pressure or control over them.

Think of empowering people instead of controlling them when you use observation to exert influence over them. Make an effort to comprehend their wants, drives, and ambitions; then, utilize this understanding to help and encourage them while they pursue their objectives. Instead of focusing just on your own interests, try to reach a solution that will benefit all parties.

3.6.5 Ongoing Self-Evaluation and Development

Ethical observation necessitates ongoing introspection and development. Evaluate your own motives, deeds, and effects on other people on a regular basis. Think about asking for input from reliable people who can offer an unbiased assessment of your moral behavior.

Take part in professional development and continuing education to enhance your comprehension of ethical issues related to observation. Make sure that your practices adhere to the highest levels of honesty and respect for others by keeping up with the latest legal and ethical requirements in your profession.

We can use the power of observation to favorably impact people while preserving their autonomy, dignity, and well-being if we preserve ethical values in our observations. Make an effort to be a responsible observer by applying your knowledge to promote harmony, establish connections, and bring about constructive change in the environment.

In   summary
When it comes to the art of subtle persuasion, observation is a useful tool, but it needs to be used carefully and ethically. Important components of ethical observation include gaining consent, protecting privacy, striking a balance between the greater good and individual rights, being open and truthful, avoiding coercion and exploitation, and regularly reflecting on oneself. By following these guidelines, we can ethically negotiate the challenges of observation and use our knowledge to constructively impact people while respecting their autonomy and dignity.

Strategic Communication

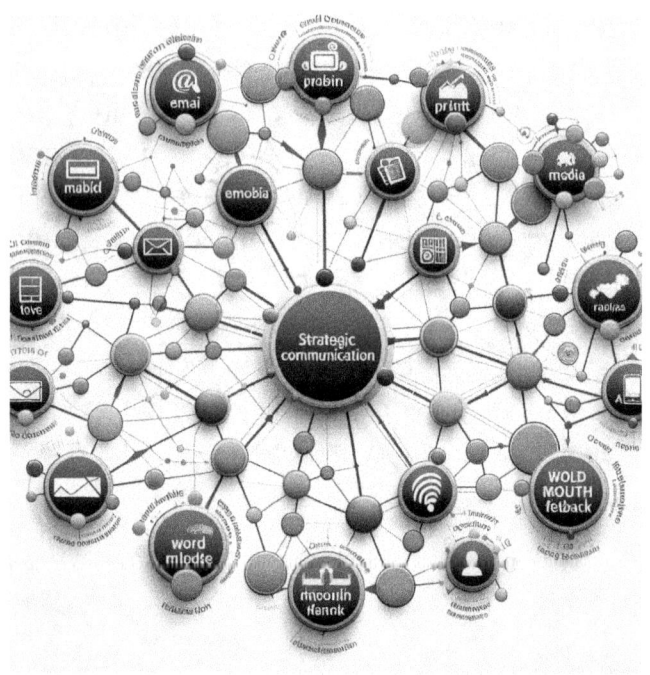

4.1 Creating Argumentative Texts

One of the key competencies in the art of subtle influence is the creation of compelling messaging. One's capacity to persuade others to adopt their viewpoints can be substantially increased by possessing the ability to communicate ideas, beliefs, and desires in an engaging and convincing way. This chapter will examine the several methods and approaches that may be used to craft messages that are not only convincing but also appropriate for the given situation and audience.

4.1.1 Recognizing the Influence of Words

Words have the ability to arouse feelings, modify behavior, and alter perceptions. When creating communications that persuade, it is essential to comprehend the power of words. The intended audience's perception and interpretation of a message can be greatly influenced by the language, tone, and style used.

The following factors should be taken into account while creating a convincing message:

4.1.1.1 Conciseness and Clarity

A convincing message should be succinct and straightforward, free of superfluous jargon or difficult vocabulary that could turn off or confuse the listener. The message becomes more approachable and comprehensible when it is expressed in plain English, which raises the likelihood that it will be well-received.

4.1.1.2 Appealing to Emotions

Making decisions is heavily influenced by emotions. A persuasive message can establish a deeper connection and resonance with the audience by appealing to their emotions. This can be accomplished by employing strong metaphors that elicit intense feelings and leave a lasting impression, vivid imagery, or anecdotes from personal experience.

4.1.1.3 Reputation and Dependability

If a compelling message originates from a reliable and reputable source, it has a higher chance of being successful. Credibility can be established by offering proof, referencing reliable sources, or making use of other people's authority and knowledge. Establishing trust with the audience is crucial to making sure that the message is taken seriously and is viewed with an open mind.

4.1.2 Adapting the Content to the Readership

Customizing a message for the target audience is essential to maximizing its persuasive power. Crafting a message that connects with different individuals or groups requires a grasp of their various values, beliefs, and priorities.

4.1.2.1 Investigation and Evaluation
It's critical to carry out in-depth target audience research and analysis prior to developing an appealing message. This entails being aware of their objectives, interests, and demographics. One can modify the message to specifically meet their issues and objectives by getting insight into their wants and desires.

4.1.2.2 Tone and Language
A convincing message should be written and delivered in a way that is consistent with the audience's values and preferences. A message intended for a younger audience, for instance, would benefit from a more relaxed and accessible tone, while one intended for a professional audience might need to use more official and technical language. By tailoring the language and tone to the audience, you may build rapport and improve the chances that the message will be understood.

4.1.2.3 Setting and Context
The persuasive power of a message can be significantly influenced by the way it is presented and framed. The message becomes more accessible and captivating when it is framed in a way that is consistent with the audience's preexisting views or

values. It's also important to take the message's delivery context into account. The relevance and impact of the message can be increased by adapting it to the particular circumstance or setting.

4.1.3 Storytelling's Power

An effective technique for creating messages that persuade is storytelling. A message can gain more impact and memory by using a story that piques the interest and feelings of the audience. Narratives possess the power to establish a bond, stimulate compassion, and motivate behavior.

4.1.3.1 Arrangement and Movement

A strong message should have a coherent structure and flow that lead the listener through an engaging story. This can be accomplished by including components like an engaging beginning, a solid storyline, and an appealing ending. The audience is more likely to be enthralled and convinced by the story being given if it is organized logically and compellingly.

4.1.3.2 Relevance and Relatability

A compelling message must be relatable and applicable to the audience's life in order to be effective. Incorporating relatable components, such as personal experiences or shared struggles, makes the message more meaningful and relatable for the audience. This makes the message more relatable and raises the possibility that the audience may be convinced by it.

Persuasive message creation is an art that demands careful attention to language, audience, and narrative devices. Learning how to write messages that persuade people is a skill that can help one influence people in subtle but powerful ways. Recall that the way in which words are expressed has just as much impact as the content they convey.

4.2   How   Effectively   to   Frame
The art of framing is a skill that may change perspectives, shift perceptions, and ultimately win people over in the complex dance of subtle influence. The skill of framing involves presenting facts or concepts in a way that affects how they are perceived and comprehended. It is a tactical instrument that gives people the power to direct decision-making processes, sway opinions, and control the   narrative.

4.2.1   The   Mentality   of   Composition
Framing has its roots in the psychology of vision and cognition in humans. Our brains are programmed to arrange information into mental models, or schemas, in order to make sense of the outside world. These schemas function as mental filters that affect our perception and comprehension of novel information. People can use these cognitive processes to their advantage and influence how others view and understand the world by carefully crafting the information they present.

An essential component of framing is the idea of "priming." The term "priming" describes the process of activating specific mental associations or notions that shape later thoughts and actions. People can influence others' brain processes and prime particular mental associations by framing information in a particular way. For instance, presenting an issue as a "challenge" as opposed to a "problem" could encourage people to take a more proactive and upbeat approach to it.

4.2.2 Techniques for Framing

There are a number of strategies that can be used to influence people and successfully frame information. Both personal and professional situations can benefit from the application of these strategies. Here are a few crucial framing strategies:

4.2.2.1 Stressing the Good

A useful framing strategy is to highlight the advantages of a situation or concept. People can foster a more positive perception and raise the possibility of acceptance or agreement by emphasizing the prospective advantages or benefits. This method works especially well when you're trying to convince someone or win them over.

4.2.2.2 Applying Analogies and Metaphors

Analogies and metaphors are effective tools for framing information. People can facilitate others' understanding and acceptance of difficult or new concepts by drawing comparisons between them and more relevant or known concepts. Metaphors and analogies have the power to conjure feelings, condense difficult concepts into manageable chunks, and enhance their persuasiveness and memorability.

4.2.2.3 Giving Background and Context

How information is interpreted can be greatly influenced by placing it in a particular context or by giving pertinent background information. People have the power to control the narrative and direct the comprehension of others by providing facts or information in a selected manner. This method is frequently applied in storytelling, as the previous knowledge and context aid in crafting an engaging and convincing story.

4.2.2.4 Recognizing and Responding to Rebuttals

Proactively addressing potential objections or counterarguments is an essential part of effective framing. People can prevent resistance and raise the possibility of acceptance by identifying and resolving any possible worries or objections. This method exhibits comprehension and empathy, which can increase trustworthiness.

4.2.3 The Framing's Ethical Aspects

Even though framing is a potent weapon for persuasion, it is important to think about the moral implications of using it. Information framing can have important effects that are both beneficial and harmful. Transparency, sincerity, and a sincere care for other people's welfare are necessary for ethical framing.

It is imperative to steer clear of fraudulent or manipulative framing strategies that take advantage of cognitive biases or misrepresent the truth. Rather, the goal of ethical framing should be to present factual and impartial information so that people can make decisions based on a thorough comprehension of the circumstances.

4.2.4 Using Framing in Day-to-Day Activities

The power of framing is ubiquitous in everyday life and is not limited to the domains of politics and business. Through comprehending and utilizing the framing principles, people can improve their ability to communicate, forge closer bonds with others, and have a beneficial impact on others.

Framing is a useful tool in interpersonal relationships to promote understanding, settle disputes, and fortify emotional bonds. Conversations can be more peaceful and encouraging when they are framed with an emphasis on empathy, reciprocity, and common objectives.

Framing is a tool that can be used in the workplace to influence decision-making processes, manage conflicts, and inspire and encourage teams. Leaders may create a productive and healthy company culture by presenting obstacles as learning opportunities, highlighting the group advantages of particular acts, and giving background and context.

Framing is a tool that advocates for causes, shapes public opinion, and promotes social change in public and social contexts. People can organize support and unite others around a shared cause by framing issues in a way that speaks to their values, emotions, and goals.

4.2.5 The Durability of Framing
Framing has the power to change people's

opinions, sway judgments, and have a long-lasting effect. People can become more compelling influencers, adept communicators, and knowledgeable power dynamics navigators by learning the art of framing.

But immense power also entails great responsibility. It is essential to approach framing with honesty, compassion, and a sincere wish to bring about constructive change. People can leverage the power of framing to create trust, encourage collaboration, and significantly improve their personal and professional lives by employing ethical and responsible framing practices.

We will discuss rapport-building and trust-building as another critical component of strategic communication in the following section. We will explore the complexities of human connection, the psychology of trust, and useful techniques for building solid bonds based on understanding and respect.

4.3 Developing a Relationship and Trust

Establishing rapport and trust are fundamental elements of subtle influence. Building a relationship and a foundation of trust is essential to successfully persuading people to agree with you. We'll look at a number of methods and approaches in this chapter that you can use to build rapport and trust with people you engage with.

4.3.1 Empathy's Power

Establishing rapport and trust can be facilitated by demonstrating empathy. You may foster a sense of connection and understanding between people by truly understanding their viewpoints and placing yourself in their position. People are more likely to trust you and be persuaded by you when they feel heard and understood.

Active listening is essential for fostering empathy. Be mindful of nonverbal clues as well as vocal ones, and show that you genuinely want to hear what other people have to say. Providing a deeper connection can also be achieved by reflecting back on their thoughts and emotions. Being empathetic means that you appreciate and honor the feelings and experiences of the other person, and this can greatly contribute to the development of trust.

4.3.2 Genuineness and Openness

In order to establish trust, authenticity and transparency are essential components. People who communicate honestly and openly are more likely to be trusted. Building credibility and cultivating trust can be facilitated by being truthful about your goals and driving forces.

Achieving a balance between strategic disclosure and transparency is crucial, though. Giving up too much too quickly can be overwhelming and work against you as a leader. As an alternative, think about progressively providing pertinent information that fits the requirements and interests of the other person. With this strategy, you may gradually establish trust while staying true to yourself.

4.3.3 Dependability and Consistency

It takes consistency and dependability to build trust. When you regularly fulfill your obligations and fulfill your promises, people will see you as a reliable and trustworthy person. This constancy lays a strong foundation for impact.

In order to exhibit dependability, it's critical to establish reasonable expectations and only take on obligations that you can honor. You build a reputation for reliability by regularly keeping your word, adhering to agreements, and meeting deadlines. Not only will this reputation increase your power, but it will also make people more confident in you.

4.3.4 Communication Through Nonverbal Means

Forging a connection and gaining trust through nonverbal communication is crucial. Oftentimes, our tone of voice, facial expressions, and body language can communicate ideas more effectively than words alone. Developing a pleasant and reliable impression can be facilitated by being aware of your nonverbal signs.

Building rapport can be facilitated by keeping eye contact, projecting an open and carefree body language, and imitating the other person's movements. Furthermore, speaking with clarity and confidence while focusing on your tone of voice can increase your reputation and dependability.

4.3.5 Establishing Mutual Understanding

Discovering points of agreement is a good

method to build rapport and confidence. People are more inclined to connect with you and believe in your intentions when they see areas of similarity and shared interests. Seek out points of similarity, such as similar goals, ideals, or experiences, and use these to establish rapport.

Finding common ground can be facilitated by listening intently and providing open-ended inquiries. You may foster mutual understanding and connections with people by being interested in their perspectives and experiences. Developing these areas of common interest can help you and the other person become closer and more trustworthy.

4.3.6 Respect and Patience
Establishing rapport and trust requires traits like patience and respect. Your efforts may be hampered if you move too quickly or ignore the boundaries set by the other person. It's critical to exercise patience and let the partnership grow organically.

It's also essential to respect the autonomy and viewpoints of others. Refrain from forcing your opinions on others or directing the discussion to further your goals. Instead, promote an atmosphere of respect for one another and candid communication. You establish a secure environment for trust to grow when you appreciate and value the opinions of others.

Establishing rapport and trust are fundamental components of subtle influence. You can build deep relationships and improve your capacity to influence others by utilizing techniques like empathy, authenticity, consistency, nonverbal communication, finding common ground, patience, and respect. Recall that the art of subtle influence is about creating sincere connections based on mutual respect and trust rather than about controlling or subduing other people.

4.4 Diplomatic Language: An Art Form
Language becomes a potent tool in the complex dance of power that may either strengthen or weaken one's authority. The skill of diplomatic language is efficiently communicating ideas while preserving peace and averting confrontation. The subtleties of diplomatic language are examined in this chapter, along with how to use them to successfully negotiate the intricate web of power relations.

4.4.1 The Power of Words Words have the ability to persuade opinions, affect feelings, and change perceptions. When it comes to subtle impact, word choice becomes crucial. The skill of diplomatic language lies in its capacity to transmit ideas with tact and precision while avoiding offense or raising suspicions. The speaker must strike a careful balance between diplomacy and assertiveness, carefully choosing their words to get the desired result.

4.4.2 Preserving Objectivity Neutrality is one of the fundamental tenets of diplomatic discourse. People can negotiate delicate subjects without offending others by avoiding strong beliefs or biases. This is especially crucial when interacting with those in positions of power, since any perceived slight to their morals or beliefs may provoke resistance or negative fallout. Speaking in a diplomatic manner permits people to voice their ideas and opinions while still being mindful of and respectful of the viewpoints of others.

4.4.3 The Euphemism Craft

A useful tactic in diplomatic discourse is euphemism. It makes it possible for people to communicate delicate or maybe offensive ideas in a way that is easier to understand. One way to lessen the effect of words while still getting the point across is to replace harsh or direct language with more subtle or indirect terms. When discussing delicate subjects or offering helpful criticism, euphemism can be quite helpful.

4.4.4 Empathy and Active Listening

Beyond only using words, diplomatic language also involves listening intently and showing empathy. People can adapt their language to resonate with their audience by genuinely understanding the needs, issues, and viewpoints of others. To make sure that the message is heard and understood as intended, active listening techniques like paraphrasing, clarifying, and reflecting are needed. Empathy enables people to emotionally connect with others, which promotes rapport and trust.

4.4.5 Communication Through Nonverbal Means

The use of nonverbal clues in diplomatic language is important. Subtle cues such as body language, tone of voice, and facial expressions can support or contradict what is said. People who are adept at using diplomatic language are aware of these nonverbal clues and make sure that their own body language supports the message they want to convey. It is possible to come across as credible and confident by keeping a cool head.

4.4.6 Forging ties and discovering points of agreement

Conveying messages is only one goal of diplomatic language; other goals include establishing rapport and creating common ground. Unity and cooperation can be fostered by individuals focusing on common ideals, objectives, or passions. This strategy enables the formation of coalitions and alliances, in which several parties collaborate to achieve a shared goal. Compromise and negotiation are essential for productive partnerships, and they are facilitated by diplomatic language.

4.4.7 Putting an End to Conflict
Human interaction will always involve conflict, but diplomatic language offers a way to manage and settle disputes amicably. People can defuse hostile circumstances and promote cooperation by using active listening, empathy, and a neutral tone. When people use diplomatic language, they are encouraged to put more effort into coming up with solutions that benefit all parties rather than getting into arguments or power conflicts.

4.4.8 Diplomatic Language Ethics
Even though diplomatic language has many uses, it is important to think about its ethical ramifications. It is improper to employ diplomatic language in a manipulative or dishonest way. Rather, its objectives ought to be to cultivate comprehension, establish connections, and encourage favorable results. The use of diplomatic language should be guided by ethical considerations to ensure that it is used honorably and with respect for other people.

4.4.9 Developing Proficiency in Diplomatic Language

Self-awareness and practice are necessary for diplomatic language competency. People can develop these abilities by proactively asking for criticism, thinking critically about how they communicate, and consistently improving the language they use. People can pick up tactics from experienced leaders, diplomats, and negotiators and modify them for their own situations.

4.4.10: Using Diplomatic Words in Daily Situations

There is more to the art of diplomatic language than just politics and diplomacy. It can be used in social situations, the workplace, and interpersonal interactions, among other areas of daily life. People who are skilled at using diplomatic language can improve their ability to communicate, forge closer bonds with others, and deftly handle power situations.

In summary, the ability to speak diplomatically is an essential trait in the field of subtle influence. It enables people to effectively communicate their messages, uphold their objectivity, and forge connections with others. Through the skill of diplomatic language, people can navigate power dynamics, settle disputes, and accomplish their goals while promoting moral behavior and healthy relationships.

Navigating Power Structures

5.1 Recognizing Influential People and Power Brokers

Finding the major players and influencers who control the dynamics of influence is crucial in the complex dance of power. These people have the power to direct decisions, manage resources, and dictate how things will unfold. You can strategically position yourself to negotiate the intricate web of power and form alliances that will advance your own goals by being aware of their responsibilities and motivations.

5.1.1 Perception's Power

Prior to learning how to spot important people and influencers, it's important to understand how perception works. Although those in positions of power frequently give off the impression that they are strong and in charge, this may not always be the case. It is critical to examine the dynamics at work and look past outward manifestations.

5.1.2 Revealing the Covert Power Brokers

Even though some people may occupy official positions of authority, there are frequently unsung heroes who exert a great deal of influence in the background. Despite the fact that these people lack titles or formal positions, the power structure depends heavily on them because of their connections, expertise, and capacity for persuasion. It takes good observational skills and an awareness of the social dynamics at work to spot these unseen forces.

5.1.3 Charting the Terrain of Power

Mapping the power landscape is crucial for identifying important people and brokers of power. Analyzing the formal and informal networks present in a particular area is necessary for this. Gaining insight into the power dynamics at work can be achieved by comprehending the partnerships, alliances, and rivalries that exist between individuals and groups.

Determine who the people in formal positions of authority are first. These could be managers, CEOs, or community or organizational leaders. Even though their influence may be obvious, it's just as crucial to recognize individuals with less official sway. Despite not holding formal titles, these people have the power to influence choices and opinions through their connections, skills, or charm.

5.1.4 Noting Influence Patterns

It's critical to look for patterns of impact in order to pinpoint important actors and influencers. Keep an eye on who is given counsel, whose views are considered when making decisions, and who has access to important data. These patterns have the ability to identify the key players in a particular setting.

Furthermore, take note of the ways in which power is allocated and shared among various people and organizations. Exist power structures based on relationships, hierarchy, or expertise? Recognizing these trends will enable you to pinpoint the major players and influence brokers in the system.

5.1.5 Making Use of Social Capital Finding the important actors and influencers is just the beginning. It is essential to establish connections and take advantage of social capital in order to successfully negotiate power structures. The networks, relationships, and connections people have that they may use to access opportunities, resources, and information are referred to as social capital.

Creating alliances with influential people and power brokers can give you access to resources, assistance, and insightful information. But it's crucial to approach these partnerships with sincerity and a sincere desire to achieve win-win solutions. Establishing enduring relationships that will enable you to successfully negotiate the intricate realm of power dynamics requires developing rapport and trust.

5.1.6 How to Map Influence Effectively

An effective method for locating influential people and power brokers is influence mapping. It entails graphically illustrating the influence, dynamics, links, and interconnections within a certain setting. You can obtain a thorough grasp of who is in a position of influence, how decisions are made, and where those opportunities are by outlining the power structure.

The first step in creating an influence map is figuring out who the important people and organizations are in the system. Examine their connections, domains of influence, and relationships after that. Research, observations, and interviews can all be used to accomplish this. You can obtain a more comprehensive understanding of the power dynamics and pinpoint the influential individuals and power brokers by visualizing these dynamics.

5.1.7 Modifying Techniques for Various Situations

It is crucial to remember that there is no one-size-fits-all method for identifying influential people and power brokers. Depending on the situation, power relations within a community, an organization, or a political system can change dramatically. As such, it is imperative that you modify your tactics and methods appropriately.

Formal positions of authority may have the most influence in some situations, but hidden influencers may have a big impact in others. You may adapt your strategy to successfully negotiate power hierarchies and form alliances with influential individuals and power brokers by being aware of the particular dynamics of each situation.

In conclusion, one of the most important skills in learning the art of subtle influence is recognizing significant people and power brokers. Through comprehending power dynamics, identifying patterns of influence, and utilizing social capital, you may adeptly navigate the intricate web of power and form partnerships that will propel your personal goals. Recall that the dance of power demands both dexterity and strategic thinking. You can enter the stage of influence with confidence by recognizing the important characters and influence brokers.

5.2 Building Relationships That Benefit Both Parties

Building relationships that benefit both parties is an essential skill for anyone hoping to become an expert at the delicate dance of power. The capacity to form coalitions and alliances can provide people with the clout and backing they need to negotiate intricate power dynamics and accomplish their objectives. The methods and approaches for establishing these kinds of connections are examined in this chapter, with a focus on the significance of reciprocity, trust, and strategic cooperation.

5.2.1 The Influence of Faith

Any effective relationship is built on trust, but this is especially true when it comes to subtle influence. When confidence is lacking, coalitions break down, and cooperation becomes less likely. Establishing credibility necessitates constancy, dependability, and an authentic dedication to the welfare of others. Since broken pledges quickly erode confidence, it is imperative to act with integrity and fulfill obligations.

It is essential to actively and sympathetically listen to the wants and worries of others in order to build trust. People can build rapport and create a secure space for open discussion by really demonstrating interest and understanding. Transparency and honesty are also important for establishing trust because deceiving people or hiding information can undermine trust and strain relationships.

5.2.2 Mutual Aid and Cooperation
Building partnerships that benefit both parties requires a careful balance of give and take. Building coalitions requires reciprocity because people are more inclined to support those who have previously been kind or helpful to them. People can cultivate a sense of reciprocity and goodwill by providing value and help to others, which paves the way for future cooperation.

Working together is a great way to form coalitions and accomplish common objectives. Individuals can expand their impact and leverage their collective capabilities by combining their resources, knowledge, and skills. Effective communication, flexibility, and a desire to discover common ground are necessary for collaboration. Collaborations must be approached with a mutually beneficial perspective, looking for win-win solutions that meet the requirements and interests of all parties.

5.2.3 Creating Bridges Rather Than Walls

It is essential to have an inclusive mindset and actively look for chances to forge connections with people if you want to master the art of subtle influence. This entails interacting with people who have different origins, viewpoints, and power structures. People can access new sources of knowledge, support, and influence by growing their network and developing relationships with a diverse spectrum of people.

Effectively managing differences and navigating confrontations are also necessary for building bridges. Any relationship will inevitably experience conflict, but it can also present a chance for development and alliance strengthening. Through the use of empathy, attentive listening, and a readiness to discover shared interests, people can turn disagreements into chances for cooperation and comprehension.

5.2.4 Emotional Intelligence's Function

Building connections based on mutual benefit requires emotional intelligence. It entails having the capacity to identify, comprehend, and effectively control one's own emotions as well as those of others. People may manage the complexity of human connection, establish rapport, and create trust by honing their emotional intelligence.

Empathy, a crucial aspect of emotional intelligence, is necessary for establishing and maintaining healthy relationships. People can develop stronger bonds and a sense of understanding by placing themselves in other people's shoes and learning about their viewpoints and feelings. By adapting their approach to the needs and motives of others, people with empathy can increase the likelihood of effective collaboration.

5.2.5 Fostering Durable Connections

Building connections that benefit both parties is a continuous process that needs to be nurtured and maintained. Building long-term connections requires time and effort since they can offer a strong base of influence and support.

Relationship maintenance requires constant engagement and communication. This may entail communicating often, exchanging information, and looking for joint venture opportunities. It's equally critical to acknowledge and celebrate other people's accomplishments and provide help when they need it. People can cultivate loyalty and commitment by exhibiting genuine concern and interest in the welfare of others.

In summary, developing relationships that benefit both parties is essential to being skilled at the art of subtle influence. Building strong alliances and coalitions requires a number of crucial components, including reciprocity, trust, teamwork, emotional intelligence, bridge-building, and long-term cultivation. People can achieve their goals and build a network of influence and support by knowing and using these tactics to traverse power hierarchies skillfully.

5.3 Bargaining and Making Compromises

Compromise and negotiation are two crucial abilities in the subtle influence technique. It is often vital to identify common ground and come to mutually beneficial agreements in the complex dance of power. This chapter examines the methods and approaches that can be used to negotiate the precarious give-and-take equilibrium.

5.3.1 The Ability to Persuade

Understanding the wants and ambitions of others and coming up with a solution that works for everyone involved are the true goals of negotiation, rather than just focusing on getting what you want. An essential part of this process is persuasion. You can raise your chances of getting a good result by making strong arguments and appealing to other people's interests.

Thorough preparation and a thorough comprehension of the goals and worries of the people you are negotiating with are essential for effective persuasion. You can craft your arguments to appeal to the needs and ideals of your opponents by carrying out an in-depth study and obtaining pertinent data.

5.3.2 Establishing rapport and trust

The cornerstone of a fruitful negotiation is trust. Finding common ground requires open and honest communication, which is difficult to create in the absence of trust. Establishing credibility requires exhibiting honesty, dependability, and a sincere desire to come to a mutually beneficial agreement.

Another important factor in negotiation is rapport. Building a cordial and courteous rapport with the opposing party fosters an atmosphere that is favorable to fruitful dialogue. Establishing rapport requires a combination of skills, including empathy, active listening, and the capacity to recognize and comprehend the viewpoints of others.

5.3.3 Discovering Win-Win Remedies

Finding win-win solutions that meet the needs of all parties involved is the art of negotiation, not winning at any cost. Thinking beyond the box and exploring creative options are necessary for this. You can find solutions that take into account the worries of both parties by concentrating on shared objectives and passions.

In negotiations, compromise is frequently required. In order to come to a consensus, compromises and a middle ground must be found. But it's crucial to approach compromise strategically and make sure that any concessions are just and equitable. To prevent overcompromise, it is also essential to keep a clear grasp of your own priorities and goals.

5.3.4 Handling Conflict and Challenging Circumstances
Conflict and difficult circumstances can occasionally arise during negotiations. It's critical to face these circumstances with composure and calmness. Emotions have the power to impair judgment and prevent clear communication. You may handle challenging circumstances more skillfully if you keep your composure and concentrate on the problems at hand.

In order to effectively manage conflict, communication skills and active listening are essential. Engaging in active listening allows you to show empathy and compassion for the worries and viewpoints of others. By doing so, tensions may be reduced and a cooperative environment may be fostered.

5.3.5 The Significance of Timing and Patience
Timing and patience are crucial components

in negotiation. Entering into a negotiation too soon or without enough preparation might have negative effects. It's critical to evaluate the circumstances, compile data, and meticulously prepare your strategy.

Negotiation also involves timing. By identifying turning points and taking advantage of chances, you can raise the probability that you will reach your goal. But it's crucial to proceed with caution and refrain from making snap decisions that can have unforeseen repercussions.

5.3.6 Negotiation's Ethical Considerations

Negotiation should always start with ethics first. It's critical to approach negotiations with honesty and justice, taking into account how your decisions will affect each and every party. Negotiation success can be hampered by manipulative strategies and unethical behavior, which can erode trust and harm relationships.

It is essential to remain truthful and open-minded during the negotiating process. You can promote a climate of trust and cooperation by being clear about your goals and intentions. In order to ensure that the negotiating process is carried out in a courteous and morally upright manner, it is also crucial to respect the limits and interests of others.

In conclusion, the art of subtle influence requires the ability to compromise and negotiate. Through the skills of persuasion, rapport-building, identifying win-win solutions, conflict management, and ethical concerns, you may successfully navigate the difficulties of negotiation. In the dance of power, successful negotiation is a useful skill that may help you forge alliances, settle disputes, and influence results in a way that is advantageous to all sides.

5.4 Making Use of Social Capital and Networks

One cannot undervalue the significance of networks and social capital in the complex dance of power. These priceless assets may hold the secret to opening doors, forming coalitions, and eventually gaining power. This chapter will examine the skill of utilizing social capital and networks, including their importance and how to navigate and develop them to strengthen our own subtle impact.

5.4.1: Networks' Power

The complex webs of connections that link people, groups, and organizations are known as networks. They act as intermediaries for opportunities, resources, and information. Gaining an understanding of the power dynamics in networks is essential for anyone looking to influence others. Through deliberate placement inside these networks, we can access an abundance of information, assistance, and relationships.

Finding important people and power brokers is crucial to utilizing networks efficiently. These are the people who can act as gatekeepers to important resources and who have a great deal of power inside the network. We can access opportunities and expand our own influence within the network by developing relationships with these people.

5.4.2 Establishing Social Capital

Social capital is the value that comes from networks and relationships with other people. It includes mutual trust, reciprocity, and other people's willingness to work together. It takes time and effort to develop relationships, build trust, and exhibit dependability and integrity in order to build social capital.

The practice of reciprocity is one of the best strategies to increase social capital. We foster a sense of mutual reliance and kindness by providing people in our network with help, encouragement, or important information. When used well, this can be a useful technique for persuading others and winning their support.

Keeping up a good reputation is a crucial part of developing social capital. The currency of influence is our reputation, which has a significant bearing on our capacity to take advantage of networks. By continuously exhibiting skill, moral character, and dependability, we may establish a solid reputation that will draw people to us and raise our social capital.

5.4.3 Getting Around and Developing Networks

It takes a thorough awareness of the social processes at work to navigate networks. Finding the people who have influence over others and the unofficial power structures in the network are crucial. By associating with these powerful people, we can obtain important resources and expand our own influence.

Network expansion is equally vital. We may expand our reach and boost our social capital by actively looking for new relationships and chances to interact with people outside of our current social circle. This can be accomplished by taking part in community activities, joining professional groups, or going to industry events. Our network's diversity increases our capacity for influence.

5.4.4 Fostering Genuine Connections

Although using social capital and networks strategically is important, it is also important to approach them with sincerity and a real interest in other people. It is significantly more productive to create deep connections based on mutual respect and trust than it is to use other people as stepping stones to our own objectives.

We must make the time and effort to get to know people personally if we are to build genuine relationships. Pay attention to their goals, interests, and worries. When help is needed, give it without expecting anything in return. We may create enduring relationships that will form the cornerstone of our impact by acting with sincere compassion and empathy.

5.4.5   Moral   Points   to   Remember
There are ethical issues when using networks and social capital, just like with any other subtle influence strategy. It is crucial that we exercise our power sensibly and morally, always keeping in mind how our actions could affect other people and the greater good.

When using networks, we have to be aware of the possibility of manipulation or exploitation. Integrity, honesty, and transparency must always be upheld in our dealings. By behaving morally, we can increase our network's trust and credibility and grow our influence in a sustainable and responsible way.

In conclusion, one of the most important skills in developing the art of subtle influence is utilizing networks and social capital. We may manage the complexity of human interaction and improve our capacity for influence by developing social capital, recognizing the power dynamics within networks, and fostering genuine relationships. But in order to ensure that our power is used sensibly and for the greater good, it is imperative that we approach this project with integrity and ethical considerations.

The Subtle Power of Influence

6.1 The Medici Sisters

The Queen Mother of France, Catherine de'Medici, was an expert at subtly influencing and manipulating people. Catherine was forced into the center of the French court at a young age when she was married off to Henry II of France and the powerful Medici family of Florence. Catherine skillfully negotiated the perilous seas of court politics throughout her life, securing her family's power and influence with wit, shrewdness, and strategic thinking.

6.1.1 The Formative Years

On April 13, 1519, Catherine de'Medici was born in Florence, Italy. She was the daughter of Madeleine de La Tour d'Auvergne and Lorenzo II de' Medici, Duke of Urbino. Catherine was introduced to the nuances of political scheming and the craft of diplomacy at an early age. Her schooling was centered on developing her intelligence, language skills, and political awareness.

Catherine married Henry, the second son of French King Francis I, when she was fourteen years old. In addition to being a marriage, this union represented a strategic partnership between the French crown and the wealthy

Medici family. Power disputes within the court and political unrest characterized Catherine's early years in France.

6.1.2 The Web of Influence of the Queen Mother

Following Henry II's death, Catherine was thrown into a powerful role as Queen Mother and regent for her three infant sons: Francis II, Charles IX, and Henry III. This was the period when Catherine's actual abilities to subtly sway people and manipulate situations became apparent.

Catherine made strategic connections with important figures in the French court by using her position and her understanding of the value of alliances. She skillfully built connections with foreign powers, powerful nobility, and the clergy to guarantee her family's standing and to establish her own authority.

The ability of Catherine to handle the religious strife that afflicted France in the sixteenth century is among her most noteworthy accomplishments. She was a devoted Catholic who had to deal with the difficulty of ruling a nation split between Catholics and Protestants over religious differences.

Catherine used a careful balancing act of diplomacy, negotiation, and deception to preserve her family's interests and maintain peace.

6.1.3 The Massacre on St. Bartholomew's Day

During Catherine de'Medici's rule, one of the most contentious incidents was the St. Bartholomew's Day Massacre in 1572. Thousands of Huguenots (French Protestants) were killed as a result of this incident, which happened during Margaret of Valois's wedding ceremonies.

It seems evident that Catherine was instrumental in the planning and execution of the massacre, even though historians disagree about the precise degree of her participation. The massacre served as a calculated action to strengthen Catholic authority and remove the Protestant challenge to the French monarchy.

6.1.4 Repercussions and Legacy

History in France has been influenced by Catherine de'Medici's time as Queen Mother. She was able to navigate the intricate web of court politics and preserve her family's dominance because of her skill at subtly influencing and manipulating others.

Catherine's reign saw significant advances in the arts and culture, despite her contentious policies. She was crucial in advancing the arts, helping writers, artists, and intellectuals of the day, as well as helping to shape the French Renaissance.

The legacy of Catherine de'Medici is proof of the potency of nuanced persuasion and the difficulties in negotiating authority. Her experience illustrates the fine line between individual ambition and the larger good, offering insightful advice on how to never outshine those in positions of control.

Readers will get a deeper comprehension of the methods, techniques, and moral issues related to perfecting the art of subtly influencing as they explore the complex realm of Catherine de' Medici's web of influence. Her experience serves as a warning, reminding us of the possible repercussions of using influence and power without giving it due thought.

6.2   Richelieu,   Cardinal

6.2.1   Cardinal   Richelieu's   Ascent

Few people in history have handled authority with as much grace as Cardinal Richelieu. Richelieu, who was born Armand Jean du Plessis in 1585, went on to become one of the most significant politicians in French history. His ascent to prominence was characterized by his unwavering pursuit of his own goals and astute grasp of the complexities of politics.

6.2.2   The   Clown   Prince   of   French Governance

During his time as France's senior minister to King Louis XIII, Cardinal Richelieu was known for his ability to influence political events for his own benefit. He saw that real power came from the deft manipulation of events occurring in the background rather than from overt acts of authority. Being an expert at manipulating the powerful, Richelieu made sure that the populace was unaware of his influence.

6.2.3 The   Skill   of   Delicate   Persuasion

Richelieu's strategy for influencing others was based on his in-depth knowledge of power dynamics and human nature. He understood that while overt demonstrations of power frequently sparked opposition and hostility, covert manipulation allowed him to control events without raising red flags. Through meticulous relationship-building and the use of his standing as the king's trusted counselor, Richelieu was able to influence events both inside and outside of the French court.

6.2.4 Forming Coalitions and Alliances Richelieu's ability to form coalitions and alliances in order to further his own agenda is one of his most noteworthy accomplishments. He realized that influence came from having the backing of others in addition to one's own standing. Richelieu was able to solidify his position of authority and guarantee the accomplishment of his goals by carefully associating himself with powerful people and taking advantage of their resources.

6.2.5 Handling the Court's Curiosities Richelieu lived in an era of intense political rivalry and intrigue at the French court. He had to use dexterity and tact to negotiate these dangerous waters in his capacity as chief minister. Richelieu used a range of strategies to stay in power, such as the employment of informants and spies to obtain information, propaganda to sway public opinion, and the calculated use of patronage to gain the allegiance of influential people.

6.2.6 Juggling Self-Interest with the Common Good

Although Richelieu was clearly a master at subtly influencing people, there was dispute surrounding his acts. His critics contend that his quest for power frequently came before the interests of society as a whole. Many viewed Richelieu's policies as harsh and bad for the welfare of the French people, including his concentration of power and his repression of Protestantism. Nonetheless, Richelieu thought that the state's stability and security required these actions.

6.2.7 The Cardinal Richelieu Legacy

The legacy of Cardinal Richelieu is multifaceted. Historians and academics are still debating his strategies and policies, even though he is frequently remembered as a capable statesman and politician. Though he was a cunning manipulator who put his personal authority above all else, some see him as a visionary leader who created the foundation for the modern nation-state. Whatever one's viewpoint, Richelieu's subdued influence on French politics and the art of government has had a lasting effect.

6.2.8 Cardinal Richelieu's Teachings

A great lesson on the skill of subtly influencing others can be learned from the tale of Cardinal Richelieu. His capacity to maneuver through the maze of power and turn circumstances to his benefit provides insights into the dynamics of authority and human connection. The legacy of Richelieu serves as a constant reminder of the need to strike a careful balance between individual goals and the larger good, as well as the moral ramifications of assuming positions of power. Readers are encouraged to examine how they handle influence in their own lives and to think about the insights that might be gained from Cardinal Richelieu's deft use of the shadow of authority.

6.3 The Prince of Machiavelli

6.3.1 The Prince: A Master of Subtle Persuasion

Renowned Italian Renaissance political philosopher Niccolò Machiavelli is well remembered for his influential book "The Prince." Machiavelli delves into the subtleties of power dynamics and the art of governing in this treatise, offering insightful perspectives into the world of subliminal influence. "The Prince" illuminates the tactics used by leaders to keep control and accomplish their goals, providing a master class in recognizing the fine line between manipulation and authority.

6.3.2 The Machiavellian Theory: When the Goals Outweigh the Means

Machiavelli's worldview is based on the idea that the means should always be justified. He contends that in order to seize and hold onto power, a dictator must be prepared to use any methods required. Machiavelli's Prince is a pragmatist and astute leader who knows that gaining power frequently necessitates the use of trickery, deceit, and manipulation. This Machiavellian paradigm emphasizes accomplishing desired results over upholding moral standards, challenging conventional ideas of morality and ethics.

6.3.3 Engineered Deceit: The Craft of Outward Presence

Machiavelli places a strong emphasis on the role appearances play in the use of authority. He counsels leaders to carefully create their public persona and use intentional deception to sway public opinion. Machiavelli believed that a leader should be both loved and feared, but that if one had to pick, it was safest to be feared. A ruler can effectively govern their followers and dissuade possible competitors by creating an image of strength and authority.

6.3.4 The Attribute of Adaptability: Changing with the Times

Machiavelli acknowledges that politics is a dynamic field and that leaders must modify their approaches accordingly. He contends that the ability to adapt one's strategy to the situation at hand is a necessary quality for a successful leader. Machiavelli counsels against strict commitment to morality, arguing that a leader should be prepared to give up virtue if it gets in the way of their ambition for power. Leaders are able to negotiate the intricacies of political environments and take advantage of opportunities by adopting this practical strategy.

6.3.5 Manipulation as an Art: Taking Advantage of Human Nature

The Prince of Machiavelli is a skilled manipulator who is aware of the complexities of human nature. He understands that people are motivated by their own interests and are susceptible to the wants and anxieties of others. Machiavelli counsels rulers to take advantage of these openings and manipulate the situation strategically in order to obtain the upper hand. A leader can gain the allegiance and support of others by appealing to their own self-interest, which guarantees their own position of authority.

6.3.6 The Shadowed Dance: Teachings from the Prince of Machiavelli

"The Prince" imparts insightful knowledge on the skill of subtly influencing others that is applicable to many facets of life. Machiavelli offers a distinct viewpoint on the intricacies of human interaction and the dynamics of power, despite the fact that his method may appear brutal and immoral. By examining the tactics used by Machiavelli's Prince, readers can learn more about the underlying dynamics that influence politics, relationships, and society.

The Prince by Niccol Machiavelli emphasizes the value of flexibility, strategic thinking, and perception management. It draws attention to the ethical issues that come with using power and the necessity of striking a balance between individual aspirations and the larger good. Machiavelli's method may not be for everyone, but it does serve as a reminder that influence is a complex and subtle art that necessitates careful maneuvering through the shadows.

Finally, Machiavelli's Prince serves as evidence of the continuing importance of subtle persuasion. Through a thorough reading of "The Prince," one can acquire priceless knowledge about the craft of manipulation, the intricacies of power relationships, and the moral dilemmas that occur when exercising influence. Machiavelli's teachings offer guidance to anyone attempting to maneuver through the shadows of authority, serving as a reminder that the dance of power necessitates dexterity as well as an awareness of the complex web of interpersonal relationships.

6.4   Sun   Tzu

The famous Chinese military strategist and philosopher Sun Tzu is best known for his book "The Art of War." Although Sun Tzu's teachings are mainly concerned with military strategy, they also include insightful information about the art of subtly influencing others. His ideas, which are based on an awareness of power relations and strategic thinking, offer a road map for resolving difficult circumstances and accomplishing goals.

6.4.1 A Strategic Guide to the Art of Warfare
The ageless classic "The Art of War" by Sun Tzu examines the nuances of conflict and the tactics needed to prevail. Beneath the surface, though, the ideas presented in this ancient work can be applied to many facets of life, such as power dynamics and the sphere of influence.

Knowing oneself and the enemy is one of Sun Tzu's most important lessons. He places a strong emphasis on the necessity of being self-aware, identifying one's advantages and disadvantages, and using them to one's benefit. Similar to this, mastering the art of subtle influence requires a thorough awareness of the desires, motives, and vulnerabilities of others. Understanding the forces at work allows one to arrange oneself in a way that maximizes influence.

6.4.2 The Influence of Misdirection and Deceit
Sun Tzu's teachings also emphasize how important deceit and misdirection are to success. He stresses the significance of projecting an illusion that disarms adversaries and throws them off balance—that is, appearing weak when strong and strong when weak. This idea can be used in the art of persuasion, where results can be shaped by subtly altering people's views.

Controlling the narrative and influencing others' perceptions is a key strategy in the influence game. It is possible to shape how other people view a situation or a person by carefully choosing which information to disclose or keep hidden. This kind of perception management can be employed to one's benefit, to forge partnerships, or to weaken adversaries.

6.4.3 The Value of Appropriate Time and Flexibility
Sun Tzu emphasizes how important timing and flexibility are in combat. He suggests taking advantage of chances when they present themselves and exploiting

weaknesses in rivals. This idea also applies to the art of influence, where deft action and the ability to spot pivotal times can produce noteworthy outcomes.

Influence is greatly influenced by timing, so actions taken at the appropriate time can have a greater effect. With a little observation and analysis, one can find the right time to influence others or take calculated action. Additionally, negotiating power relations requires flexibility. Increased success in persuading others is possible when tactics and methods may be modified in response to evolving conditions.

6.4.4 Striking a Balance Between Diplomacy and Force

In Sun Tzu's teachings, the proper use of force and diplomacy are emphasized. He contends that accomplishing goals without going through direct combat is the highest form of triumph. This idea is consistent with the art of subtle influence, which often finds that compulsion or force is ineffective.

The best forms of influence are those that are subtle, convincing, and based on rapport and trust. One can attain their objectives without using overt acts of power by using diplomatic language, forming alliances, and comprehending the motivations of others. In addition to maintaining ties, this strategy opens up the possibility of long-term influence and ongoing cooperation.

6.4.5 The Influence's Ethical Considerations
Even if Sun Tzu's teachings offer insightful guidance on the art of persuasion, one must always think about the moral ramifications of their choices. The greater good or the welfare of others should never be sacrificed in the name of power and influence. Maintaining integrity and making sure that one's actions are consistent with one's principles require an understanding of the bounds of ethical influence.

The lessons of Sun Tzu serve as a reminder that, similar to battle, influence must be used wisely, strategically, and with a thorough grasp of human nature. By putting his ideas into practice in the art of subtle influence, we may accomplish our goals, negotiate power dynamics skillfully, and create enduring bonds based on respect and trust.

The Shadows of Morality

7.1 The Narrow Line That Separates Influence from Manipulation

The distinction between influence and manipulation can frequently become hazy in the complex web of power dynamics. It is vital to examine the ethical issues that come up when negotiating this fragile terrain as we go deeper into the art of subtle persuasion. Mastering the dance of shadows requires an understanding of the thin line that separates influence from manipulation.

7.1.1 The Character of Influence

Fundamentally, influence is the capacity to mold the attitudes, behaviors, and choices of other people. It is an inherent component of human contact that exists to varying degrees and shapes throughout our lives. Whether we are aware of it or not, the people and situations in our immediate environment have an ongoing impact on us.

When used effectively, influence may motivate people to develop, learn, and realize their full potential. It has the power to spur development, encourage teamwork, and create a peaceful atmosphere. But influence can also be used for less honorable purposes, such as exploitation and manipulation.

7.1.2 The Influence of Goals

The underlying aim is the primary distinction between influence and manipulation. When applied morally, influence aims to elevate and empower people, promoting development and mutual gain. It is based on decency, compassion, and a sincere wish to have a constructive influence.

Contrarily, manipulation stems from a self-serving desire to exert control over others in order to further one's own interests. It entails using trickery, applying pressure, and taking advantage of weaknesses. The goal of manipulation is to further the manipulator's agenda at the expense of other people's autonomy and well-being.

7.1.3 Fostering Consent and Trust

The development of consent and trust is a vital component of ethical influence. The basis for influence to flourish is trust. It must be gained by being open, truthful, and sincere in one's concern for the welfare of others. Without trust, power loses its meaning and potency.

Another important factor in ethical influence is consent. It guarantees people the freedom to choose and decide for themselves. Influencers who are ethical respect other people's limits and agency; they want to convince rather than compel. They recognize that genuine influence is the result of a cooperative process in which both sides voluntarily participate in a win-win transaction.

7.1.4 The Significance of Openness

The foundation of ethical influence is transparency. It entails being forthright and truthful about one's goals, drives, and strategies. Ethical influencers empower people to recognize the influence they are exerting and to make informed decisions while preserving their sense of self.

On the other hand, deceit and secrecy provide the perfect environment for manipulation. Tricks used by manipulators to mask their genuine motivations include taking advantage of weaknesses and establishing an imbalance of power. The antidote to manipulation is transparency, which enables people to safeguard themselves against improper influence and reveals hidden motives.

7.1.5 Juggling Authority and Obligation

tremendous responsibility accompanies tremendous influence. Influencers that uphold ethics are aware of their power and make prudent use of it. They make an effort to make sure that their influence is in line with moral standards and the greater good since they are aware that their actions have effects.

Being aware of the possible harm that can result from unbridled influence is crucial.

Improper use of influence can result in the exploitation of weak people, the breakdown of trust, and the maintenance of unfair power relationships. In an ongoing effort to reduce these dangers, ethical influencers assess their strategies and goals.

7.1.6 The Unceasing Path of Self-Examination It takes ongoing introspection and self-examination to walk the tightrope between influence and manipulation. It necessitates a constant assessment of one's aims, strategies, and motivations. Since they understand that the dance of shadows is a lifetime adventure, ethical influencers are dedicated to personal development and self-awareness.

Ethical influencers can spot and deal with any manipulation tendencies by developing self-awareness. They make an effort to make sure that their impact is based on honesty and regard for others by trying to match their deeds with their principles.

7.1.7 Adopting a Moral Perspective It is important to keep in mind that ethical influence is a potent weapon for positive change as we examine the art of subtle influence. We may negotiate power relations with integrity and empathy if we can see the thin line that separates influence from manipulation. Fairness, respect, and the greater good are the guiding principles of a society where the dance of shadows is governed by ethical influence, which also empowers others and promotes collaboration.

7.2 The Morality of Authority and Power

Ethical issues are vital in defining the limits of influence within the complex web of power and authority. In order to fully understand the art of subtle persuasion, we must consider the moral ramifications of exercising authority and power. This chapter explores the moral conundrums that come up when negotiating the shadow of influence, emphasizing the fine line that must be drawn between selfish interests and the greater good.

7.2.1 Power's Responsibilities

Power and authority entail a significant amount of responsibility. People with the power to influence others need to be aware of the effects that their actions can have on other people and society at large. Power must be used responsibly, with empathy, and with a thorough awareness of the potential repercussions. This is a requirement of ethical principles.

7.2.2 The Enticement of Abuse

The seduction of power can be overwhelming, causing people to abuse their position for their own benefit. Nonetheless, the morally upright course necessitates eschewing such allures and utilizing authority for the benefit of others. It's important to keep in mind that influence should be utilized for empowerment and uplift rather than manipulation and exploitation.

7.2.3 Juggling One's Own Interests with the Greater Good

A major moral conundrum for those in positions of responsibility is balancing the interests of the greater good with one's own. Although self-interest is inherent, ethical influence necessitates taking other people's wellbeing and the long-term effects of one's activities into consideration. The secret to subtle influence is to figure out how to match individual objectives with societal advancement.

7.2.4 Accountability and Transparency

Being accountable for one's conduct and upholding transparency are crucial components of ethical influence. People in positions of authority should be transparent and truthful about their goals, making sure that their words and deeds match. The ethical underpinnings of influence can be reinforced and trust can be established by cultivating a culture of accountability and transparency.

7.2.5 Honoring Individuality and Consent

In the context of influence, respecting the autonomy and consent of others is a cornerstone ethical concept. Realizing that everyone has the freedom to make their own decisions is essential. Encouraging others to exercise their autonomy and ensuring that permission is freely provided without manipulation or coercion are two aspects of ethical influence.

7.2.6 Preventing Injury and Inadvertent Repercussions

A thorough evaluation of the possible harm and unforeseen repercussions of one's actions is necessary for ethical influence. It is crucial to weigh the advantages and disadvantages of exercising authority and power and taking action to reduce negative effects and increase favorable ones. The goal of ethical influence is to improve society and individuals overall.

7.2.7 Seeking Justice and Fairness

Justice and fairness must be the cornerstones of every effort to influence ethics. Being fair to people and not favoritizing or discriminating against them is crucial to preserving the integrity of influence. The goal of ethical influence is to level the playing field so that everyone has an equal chance to prosper.

7.2.8 The Ongoing Process of Ethical Development

Being an ethical influencer is a journey, not a destination, that requires constant development and introspection. It necessitates a dedication to understanding, modifying, and improving one's method of influence. People can work to become more ethical influencers and improve the world by continuously considering and analyzing the ethical consequences of their activities.

The route of influence is illuminated by ethical principles, which act as guiding lights in the shadows of power and authority. It is crucial to keep in mind that true power comes from the capacity to empower, uplift, and effect positive change rather than from the ability to manipulate or exploit others as we negotiate the complexity of the art of subtle influence. We may master the dance of influence with integrity and leave a lasting impression on the world by adhering to ethical ideals.

7.3 Juggling Individual Benefits with the Common Good

One must walk the fine line between self-interest and the greater good in the complex dance of subtle persuasion. Even though self-interest frequently drives the quest for power and influence, it is crucial to think about the bigger picture and how our actions may affect other people. This chapter examines the moral issues that come up when using authority shadows, stressing the significance of keeping a moral compass in mind when practicing the art of subtly influencing others.

7.3.1 The Moral Catch-22

The moral conundrum that appears when participating in the dance of power must be faced. On the one hand, it might be alluring to pursue one's own interests and goals, especially when they appear to be in line with the intended result. But it's important to consider the effects of our choices and the possible harm they could bring to other people. We must be committed to acting in a way that maintains ethical ideals and carefully consider our motivations in order to strike a balance between our personal gain and the greater good.

7.3.2 The Significance of Goals

In the world of subtle influence, our intentions are a big part of what makes our actions moral. Even though the results of our influence could be positive, we still need to consider the motivations behind our decisions. Are we motivated by a sincere desire to have a beneficial influence, or are we pursuing power for the sake of achieving personal glory? We may make sure that ethical concerns steer our influence by ensuring that our aims are in line with the larger good.

7.3.3 The Influence of Compassion

A guiding concept in striking a balance between one's own interests and the greater good is empathy. We can have a better understanding of the possible outcomes of our actions by placing ourselves in the position of others. By considering the effects on people and communities, empathy enables us to make sure that our influence does not come at the expense of other people's wellbeing. We can walk through the shadows of authority with compassion and integrity if we practice empathy.

7.3.4 Moral Choice-Making

Making moral decisions is an essential ability for anyone hoping to become an expert at subtly influencing others. It entails making a conscious decision to behave morally and carefully weighing the possible repercussions of our choices. Making ethical decisions necessitates thinking through the long-term effects of our decisions and putting the welfare of others ahead of our own interests. We may make sure that our influence is both morally and practically sound by integrating ethical issues into our decision-making process.

7.3.5 The Function of Responsibility
A key element in striking a balance between individual benefit and the larger good is accountability. It entails accepting accountability for the results of our deeds and being prepared to deal with the fallout from our impact. Holding oneself responsible shows that we have integrity and that we are dedicated to acting morally. In addition to preventing the abuse of power, accountability makes sure that our influence is based on moral standards.

7.3.6 The Effects Over Time
Acknowledging the long-term consequences of our activities is essential when weighing the trade-off between self-interest and the greater good. Even though certain decisions can pay

off right away, others might have long-term effects that threaten the fundamental basis of power. We can create a lasting legacy of ethical influence by putting the greater good ahead of our immediate needs.

7.3.7 Seeking to Have an Ethical Impact Pursuing ethical influence necessitates a dedication to ongoing introspection and development. It entails assessing our goals and behaviors on a regular basis, getting input from others, and growing from our errors. We may walk the shadows of authority with integrity and make sure our influence serves the greater good by adopting a growth mindset and being committed to ethical behavior.

Ethical leadership is characterized by the capacity to strike a balance between one's own interests and the greater good in the complex dance of power and influence. We may use the shadows of authority with honesty, empathy, and a dedication to changing the world for the better by accepting this fine balance.

7.4 The Repercussions of Immoral Influence

The distinction between morally right and wrong behavior can frequently become hazy in the complex dance of influence and power. It's important to understand the possible repercussions of overstepping the line while using the art of subtle influence, even if it may be a very effective instrument for accomplishing both professional and personal objectives. The ramifications of unethical influence can be extensive, affecting not just the individuals involved but also the larger social structure in which they function.

7.4.1 Undermining Credibility and Trust The loss of credibility and trust is one of the worst effects of unethical influence. People run the danger of losing their reputation and the trust that others have in them when they use deceptive or manipulative methods to get what they want. Any successful relationship, whether personal or professional, is built on trust, and once it is lost, it can be difficult to regain. Losing trust may have long-term effects that affect relationships and future possibilities, in addition to the current circumstances.

7.4.2 Establishing a Distrustful Culture

In addition to having an impact on the people directly involved, unethical influence can foster a culture of mistrust in a community or organization. People may become suspicious and cynical of others who exhibit deceptive conduct, which can hinder communication and teamwork. People may grow defensive and reluctant to divulge information or ideas in such a setting, impeding advancement and limiting creativity. A culture of mistrust can have negative effects on an organization's or community's general success and well-being.

7.4.3 Isolating People and Breaking Relationships

Relationships can be strained, and people can feel alienated by unethical influence. Feelings of betrayal and animosity can result when people put their own interests ahead of other people's needs. Individuals who have been tricked or misled could turn away from the influencer, severing ties and depriving themselves of assistance. Broken relationships can have long-term effects that go beyond the immediate repercussions, affecting future cooperation and development prospects.

7.4.4 Undermining Engagement and Morale

An organization's or community's involvement and morale can be severely impacted by unethical influence. Those who believe they are being used for someone else's benefit or that their interests are not being taken into consideration may become disillusioned and disengaged. This may lead to lower output, higher employee attrition, and a general drop in morale. Any group or organization's success and sustainability may suffer from the effects of poor morale and disengagement.

7.4.5 Risks to One's Reputation and Law

Participating in unethical influence might put one's reputation and legal standing in jeopardy. Individuals may face legal repercussions, including lawsuits or criminal charges, contingent on the type of unethical action. Furthermore, harm to one's reputation may have enduring consequences, influencing prospects and connections in the future. There is no assurance that repairing a damaged reputation will be easy, and it can take a long time. An individual's personal and professional life may be significantly impacted by the repercussions of legal and reputational concerns.

7.4.6 Long-Term Effects and Ethical Issues

The temptation to use unethical influence to further one's aims may be strong, but it's important to think about the long-term effects of such behavior. Our judgments and deeds should be guided by ethical principles since they not only mold our own personalities but also the society in which we inhabit. Beyond the immediate issue, unethical influence can have an impact on our relationships, our reputation, and the general well-being of our communities. We can build a more peaceful and sustainable world by upholding moral values and ethically mastering the art of subtle influence.

To sum up, the ramifications of unethical influence are extensive and can significantly affect people, relationships, organizations, and communities. Through acknowledging the possible repercussions and adhering to moral values, we can skillfully maneuver through the shadow of influence and make a constructive and enduring difference in the world.

The Dance of Power

8.1 Recognizing Power Relations and Organizational Culture

Anyone trying to negotiate the murky waters of authority must have a thorough awareness of the culture and power dynamics at work in the complex web of organizational dynamics. A group or institution's collective identity is shaped by its common values, beliefs, and practices, which are referred to as organizational culture. On the other hand, power dynamics include how authority is used and distributed within an organization.

8.1.1 Organizational Culture's Impact

The unseen thread that unites the individuals in an organization is its organizational culture. It establishes the standards for behavior, values, and decision-making. Anyone trying to influence others within the system needs to have a thorough understanding of the subtleties of organizational culture.

The official and unofficial guidelines that control conduct are one facet of company culture. Informal rules are the unspoken conventions that direct daily encounters, whereas formal rules are usually found in policies and procedures. People can move more skillfully through the organizational landscape by paying attention to and comprehending these guidelines.

The common values and beliefs of the company are another crucial component of its culture. Individuals' attitudes and conduct within the organization are shaped by these ideals. People can become more credible and influential by matching their words and deeds with the norm.

Additionally, the language and symbols employed inside the firm are frequently manifestations of organizational culture. People can interact with one other and establish rapport by using the organization's symbols and speaking its language.

8.1.2 Revealing the Power Structure Within an organization, power dynamics dictate who can influence others, who has access to resources, and who makes decisions. Anyone trying to negotiate the murky waters of authority needs to understand these power relations.

The official organizational hierarchy is one facet of power relations. The authority structure and reporting lines are shown in this hierarchy. It is possible for people to recognize important decision-makers and power holders by knowing the formal hierarchy.

Formal roles do not, however, influence power dynamics exclusively. Within organizations, there are also unofficial hierarchies of power. These unofficial power structures may be founded in experience, connections, or individual influence. Through recognizing these unofficial power structures, people can use their affiliations and connections to their advantage and increase their influence.

Within an organization, resource distribution has an impact on power dynamics as well. People in charge of resources frequently have a lot of influence. People can locate possible sources of power and strategically align themselves with those in charge by knowing how resources are distributed.

Furthermore, the capacity to influence others affects power relations. Individuals with good communication and persuasion skills frequently hold more sway inside the company. People can improve their capacity to negotiate power dynamics and exercise influence by developing these abilities.

8.1.3 Handling Power Dynamics and Organizational Culture
In order to negotiate power dynamics and organizational culture effectively, individuals need to take a strategic approach. Here are

some tactics to think about:

Observe and Pay Attention: Give careful attention to the dynamics occurring within the organization. Be mindful of the shared ideals, the formal and unwritten regulations, and the power relationships that are in place. This will offer insightful information for navigating the corporate environment.

Develop Relationships: Foster connections with important figures in the company. Determine who is influential and powerful, then make an effort to build a relationship with them. Developing ties and alliances will help you better negotiate power dynamics and win people over to your ideas.

Adapt and Flex: Be aware that power relations and company culture can change depending on the circumstances. Be flexible and adaptive in your approach, modifying your plans to suit the particular situation. This will make you more adept at negotiating the authority shadows.

Utilize Expertise: Recognize your strengths and use them to your advantage to influence others. Establishing oneself as an important resource can help you become more credible and have more influence over decisions made within the company.

Ethical Considerations: Upholding moral principles is crucial while negotiating power relations and company culture. Keep in mind the moral conundrums that could occur and make an effort to behave in a way that respects justice and honesty.

Through a comprehensive grasp of organizational culture and power dynamics, people can adeptly and skillfully maneuver through the shadows of authority. Individuals that possess these skills will be able to influence others subtly and accomplish their objectives within the framework of an organization.

8.2   Having   an   Impact

One of the most important things to learn in the complex dance of organizational politics is how to influence others. Acquiring the endorsement and confidence of higher-ups might significantly alter your professional path by providing access to novel prospects and guaranteeing that your thoughts are acknowledged and appreciated. However, it takes skill and strategic thought to negotiate the delicate dynamics of power dynamics and express your influence without going too far. We will look at practical methods in this chapter for winning over people in positions of power and influencing them upward.

8.2.1 Comprehending the Power Dynamics

Understanding the power relations in your organization is crucial before starting your influence-up journey. Determine the important individuals who have influence over decision-making processes and acknowledge the formal and informal institutions that influence them. You can deliberately arrange yourself to influence people with the ability to make significant decisions by being aware of the dynamics of power.

8.2.2 Establishing Trust and Credibility

Establishing confidence and trust with your superiors is essential to successfully influencing them. They will be more receptive to your thoughts and proposals if you can demonstrate your knowledge, expertise, and dependability. Spend some time learning about their issues and priorities so that you can match your objectives with theirs. You may build a foundation of trust that will strengthen your influence by demonstrating your genuine interest in the organization's success and your interest in their point of view.

8.2.3 Strategic Idea Presentation

Being smart in your approach is crucial when pitching ideas to higher-ups. Adjust your message to fit their communication style and preferences. Take into account their top goals and present your suggestions in a way that emphasizes how they could help the company. Show them that you have considered the possible difficulties and have workable answers by being proactive in responding to their worries. Gaining their support and buy-in is more likely when you deliver your ideas strategically.

8.2.4 Making the Most of Networks and Relationships

You can greatly increase your potential to influence higher levels in the organization by forming alliances and developing relationships with powerful people. Find ways to cooperate with influential people who wield influence over your superiors. These people are often important stakeholders. You can expand the reach of your ideas and boost your influence by making the most of your connections and networks. To ensure that your alliances are based on respect for one another and common objectives, it is imperative that you approach these partnerships with authenticity and integrity.

8.2.5: Taking Charge

Understanding your superiors' preferences and working methods and modifying your approach accordingly are key components of managing up. Pay attention to how they make decisions, communicate, and how they prefer to receive information. Adapt your interactions to suit their tastes by giving brief updates, setting up frequent check-ins, or using a certain format for information. You can improve rapport, expedite communication, and gain more clout by managing up.

8.2.6 Exhibiting Proactivity and Initiative

Supervisors value workers who are proactive and show initiative. Seek out chances to go above and beyond the duties you have been given and take on extra projects or tasks that support the objectives of your superiors. You can attract the respect and attention of individuals in positions of control by showcasing your dedication to the organization's success and your readiness to take on difficulties. But it's crucial to find a balance and make sure you don't overwork yourself or ignore your primary obligations.

8.2.7 Practicing Perseverance and Patience

Gaining influence is not always an easy task. It calls for both perseverance and patience. Acknowledge that relationships and support may be earned through repeated encounters and efforts and that transformation takes time. Along the journey, be ready for setbacks and hurdles, but maintain your resiliency and dedication to your objectives. You can eventually overcome reluctance and get the help you need by being persistent and patient.

8.2.8 Moral Points to Remember

It's critical to uphold moral principles when negotiating in the world of influence. Make sure that your behavior is consistent with the organization's ideals and that pursuing influence does not come at the expense of your integrity. Refrain from using deceptive or immoral strategies that could hurt other people or tarnish your reputation. Keep in mind that authenticity, respect, and trust are the foundations of meaningful influence.

Effective communication, strategic thinking, and a thorough understanding of power dynamics are all necessary for the delicate dance of influence. You can influence the course of your career, get the support of people in positions of power, and manage organizational politics with skill if you can master the art of influencing. If you approach this dance with integrity and a sincere desire to see the firm succeed, you'll discover that you're rising to a position of trust and influence in your workplace.

8.3 Creating Alliances and Managing Peers

Building alliances and managing colleagues are critical skills for anyone trying to negotiate the tangled web of power dynamics that is organizational politics. Building connections with coworkers on an equal footing is just as vital as exerting influence over superiors and subordinates. Peers can be useful allies or strong rivals, and knowing how to handle these relationships well can make a big difference in one's capacity to quietly influence others inside an organization.

8.3.1 The Influence of Teamwork

The foundation of forming alliances with peers is collaboration. When people collaborate to achieve a common objective, they can take advantage of each other's abilities and resources, resulting in a positive synergy for all. Building camaraderie and mutual respect through collaboration paves the way for cooperation and trust.

It is crucial to approach peer interactions with an open mind and a readiness to listen in order to collaborate with peers effectively. Actively look for chances to work together on initiatives or projects, and be open to hearing other people's viewpoints and thoughts. Fostering an inclusive environment and appreciating others' efforts will help you cultivate a collaborative culture that will inspire your colleagues to collaborate with you.

8.3.2 Establishing rapport and trust

Building partnerships and managing colleagues both require rapport and trust. Gaining people's trust requires acting in a dependable and consistent manner, as well as exhibiting expertise and honesty in your profession. Make sure your peers feel comfortable depending on you by acting with transparency and maintaining open communication.

However, sincere ties and common experiences are the foundation of rapport. Spend some time getting to know your peers personally and demonstrating an interest in their goals and lifestyles. Find common ground and have meaningful conversations to help build understanding and a sense of camaraderie.

8.3.3 Handling Rivalry and Disagreement

It is inevitable for there to be competition and conflict in any organizational context. However, maintaining a healthy balance between cooperation and healthy competition is necessary for managing peers and forming partnerships. It's critical to understand that, while competition can spur development and innovation, it should never come at the expense of strained ties or mistrust among coworkers.

When confronted with rivalry or disagreement, adopt a solution-focused attitude and show empathy for the other party. Attempt to comprehend the viewpoints and incentives of your colleagues, and search for chances to establish points of agreement and arrive at win-win solutions. You may turn rivalry into an engine for cooperation and the formation of alliances by concentrating on common objectives and interests.

8.3.4 Making the Most of Networking and Influence

Leveraging influence and networking inside the firm are other components of forming alliances with peers. Find people who are in positions of power or who have important knowledge, and look for ways to get in touch with them. Take part in deep dialogue, extend help and support, and show off your knowledge and worth.

Professional associations, industry conferences, and networking events can offer beneficial chances to broaden your network and form partnerships with colleagues outside of your current workplace. Participate fully in these gatherings, strike up conversations, and make relationships that may prove advantageous to both parties in the future.

8.3.5 Promoting a Positive Workplace Environment

Building relationships and managing colleagues includes more than just self-interest; it also entails fostering a positive workplace culture. You may establish an atmosphere where everyone feels appreciated and inspired to work together to achieve common objectives by encouraging a cooperative and supportive work environment.

Celebrate your colleagues' successes, foster an environment of open communication, and advance an appreciation and recognition culture. By fostering a healthy company culture, you can improve relationships with colleagues and foster an atmosphere that supports everyone's success and personal development.

To sum up, mastering the art of subtle influence inside an organization requires a strong foundation in alliance-building and peer management. One can manage relationships with peers and form alliances that help them exert influence and accomplish their goals by cooperating, developing rapport and trust, managing competition and conflict, using influence and networking, and fostering a positive organizational culture.

8.4: Taking the Lead in the Dark
Leaders in the complex dance of power have to learn how to lead from the shadows, influencing their subordinates, in addition to navigating the challenges of persuading peers and superiors. It takes a careful mix of subtlety and authority to lead from the shadows; leaders must use their influence without obscuring their team members. This chapter delves into the methods and approaches that leaders can use to guide and motivate their team members to excel.

8.4.1 The Influence of Understanding and Empathy
Leaders who want to lead from the shadows must first cultivate a strong sense of understanding and empathy for their subordinates. Leaders can learn a great deal about their team members' goals, motivations, and difficulties by placing themselves in their position. With the help of this knowledge, leaders can adjust their methods and communication nuances to better connect with and build trust with their subordinates.

Proficient leaders also understand the value of attentive listening. Leaders show that they value their subordinates' opinions and are committed to their success by actively listening to their worries, suggestions, and criticism. Members of the team feel more empowered as a result, and an atmosphere of candid and open communication is fostered.

8.4.2 Fostering a Helpful Environment

Leading from the shadows entails fostering an atmosphere of empowerment so that team members may own their jobs and provide their special talents and viewpoints. Leaders can accomplish this by cultivating a collaborative culture that values different points of view and encourages innovation.

Through assigning tasks and offering chances for improvement, leaders enable their staff members to take on new challenges and broaden their skill sets. This strengthens the team's capabilities and gives the members a sense of pride in their job.

8.4.3 Setting a Good Example

Leaders who operate in the background are aware of the influence of setting a good example. They set the bar high for professionalism and performance by modeling the attitudes and actions they want from their subordinates. Leading with honesty, responsibility, and a strong work ethic encourages others in the team to do the same.

Moreover, leaders who operate in the background recognize the need for humility. Giving credit where credit is due, they recognize and value the contributions made by each member of their team. This promotes cooperation and creativity, in addition to a feeling of camaraderie and respect for one another.

8.4.4 Offering Counseling and Mentoring Leaders who lead from the shadows understand how important it is to coach and guide their subordinates. They are aware that by supporting the personal and professional development of their team members, they are developing future leaders in addition to strengthening the team.

In order to help their subordinates realize their full potential, leaders should provide them with coaching, mentorship, and constructive criticism. This entails offering direction on professional growth as well as technical skills, assisting team members in navigating their career pathways, and overcoming obstacles in the process.

8.4.5 Honoring Achievement and Recognizing Work

Leading from the shadows also entails recognizing each team member's contribution and rejoicing in the group's accomplishments. Proficient leaders comprehend the significance of acknowledgment and gratitude in stimulating and encouraging their team members.

Leaders who celebrate and acknowledge accomplishments in public not only raise spirits but also foster a culture of excellence and ongoing development. This acknowledgement can come in many different forms, like verbal compliments, written praise, or even little gifts of gratitude. Making sure team members feel appreciated and acknowledged for their work is crucial.

8.4.6 Building a Culture of Psychological Safety and Trust

Psychological safety and the development of a culture of trust are top priorities for leaders who lead from the shadows. They foster an atmosphere where team members are at ease taking chances, voicing their opinions, and questioning the status quo.

Through the establishment of trust and psychological safety, leaders promote candid and open communication, teamwork, and creativity. Team members can freely voice their thoughts, ask questions, and grow from their mistakes as a result, which eventually promotes both professional and personal development.

8.4.7 Modifying Leadership Approaches Leaders who operate in the background must be flexible in their approach to leadership. Successful leaders are aware that no two people are the same and that there is no one-size-fits-all approach to leadership.

Leaders can enhance their impact and forge closer bonds with their subordinates by customizing their leadership approaches to suit their preferences and needs. This could entail giving certain team members more direction and assistance while giving others greater freedom and independence.

8.4.8 Handling Difficulties and Conflict Being a leader in the shadows has its difficulties. Within their teams, leaders could run into resistance, disagreements, or challenging circumstances. Effective leaders in these situations maintain their composure, objectivity, and calmness while attempting to identify the underlying reasons for the problems and come up with workable solutions.

Leaders show their dedication to the success and well-being of their team by confronting problems and difficulties head-on. They ensure that the team stays focused on its goals and objectives by promoting open communication, encouraging teamwork, and mediating disagreements as needed.

It takes a certain set of abilities and a profound comprehension of human dynamics to emerge from the shadows. Leaders can inspire their subordinates to achieve greatness by fostering empathy, fostering a supportive environment, setting an example, offering advice and mentoring, celebrating accomplishments, fostering trust, adjusting leadership styles, and overcoming obstacles. By doing this, they establish a cohesive and productive team that benefits from their subtle influence.

The Art of Timing

9.1 Identifying Influence-Critical Times
Timing is crucial in the complex dance of subtle impact. The difference between skilled manipulators and casual observers is their capacity to identify moments of influence. Like passing shadows, these moments might appear in a variety of ways and situations,

necessitating keen awareness and prompt action. This chapter will examine how to spot these crucial opportunities and act quickly to seize them.

9.1.1 The Perceptual Power

One of the most important factors in identifying influential moments is perception. It serves as the prism through which we view the world and molds our comprehension of the dynamics in operation. Sharpening our senses allows us to recognize minute changes in authority, spot new opportunities, and foresee possible dangers.

The sense of power is one component of perception to take into account. It is possible to determine the important individuals and power brokers in a given situation by comprehending the power dynamics within it. Through examining the distribution of authority and the ways in which people react to it, we can acquire important understandings of the current power structures and pinpoint the times at which influence can be used most successfully.

The capacity to read individuals is another facet of perception. Body language and facial expressions are examples of nonverbal cues that can disclose emotions and intentions that are hidden. We may better comprehend people's genuine intents and desires by keeping a watchful eye out for these indications, which will help us adjust our approach and influence people more successfully.

9.1.2 The Timing Dance

Within the domain of subtle effect, timing is a delicate art. It calls for an acute sense of observation as well as knowledge of the dynamics of power ebb and flow. Being aware of the changing tides and understanding when to act, when to wait, and when to strike are necessary for identifying important times of influence.

Timing requires a critical element of strategic patience. There are situations where waiting for the ideal opportunity to act is the best course of action. This necessitates both a thorough comprehension of the current circumstances and the capacity to control one's impulse to respond hastily. We can position ourselves for optimum effect and make sure that our influence is applied at the most advantageous time by practicing strategic patience.

Another important part of time is seizing the moment. There are times in the dance of influence when the power dynamics shift, offering opportunities to those who are observant enough to spot them. These possibilities could show up as a change in circumstances, a movement in alliances, or a vulnerable moment. We have the power to exert influence and sway the outcome in our favor by precisely grasping these moments.

9.1.3 The Dangers of Retaliation As vital as it is to identify windows of opportunity for influence, we also need to be aware of the backlash and unforeseen repercussions that could result from our activities. When used carelessly, influence can give rise to distrust, discontent, and even insurrection. As such, it is imperative that we exercise prudence and foresight in our actions and think through the possible consequences of our influence.

The possibility of going too far is one such hazard. It's critical to strike a careful balance between assertiveness and respect for the autonomy of others when trying to establish influence. Overexerting ourselves or stepping outside moral bounds can result in resistance and retaliation, which undermines our efforts and ruins relationships.

We also need to think about the possible effects on our trustworthiness and reputation. Our influence may be less effective in the future and damage trust if it is thought to be manipulative or self-serving. As such, when exercising our influence, it is imperative that we do it with integrity and with the greater good in mind.

9.1.4 The Craft of Modification Acknowledging pivotal times for impact necessitates the capacity to modify and refine our strategies as situations change. The terrain of the power dance is dynamic and ever-evolving, and strategies that were successful in one circumstance might not be successful in another. Maintaining our impact and negotiating the complexity of human contact require flexibility and adaptability.

Changing our communication style, rewriting our plans, or even reassessing our objectives can all be considered forms of strategy adaptation. We can keep improving our abilities and staying ahead of the always-changing currents of power by continuing to be receptive to new ideas and eager to absorb lessons from our past mistakes.

To sum up, mastering the ability to identify pivotal times for influence requires acute observation, a sense of timing, and flexibility. By being skilled at this craft, we can move through the complex dance of power with grace and accuracy, making sure that our influence is used when it is most needed. But it's important to approach influence with integrity and think through the possible outcomes of our choices. Finding the right balance between taking advantage of chances and averting potential backlash is the skill of identifying important moments for influence, which eventually enables us to use our influence wisely and effectively.

9.2   Adaptive   Patience

Timing is crucial in the complex dance of subtle impact. The difference between skilled manipulators and casual viewers is their capacity to identify pivotal moments and capitalize on them. The capacity to wait for the ideal opportunity to act, or the art of strategic patience, is nevertheless equally crucial. This chapter will examine the value of patience in influencing others and teach you how to strike a careful balance between taking action and staying still.

9.2.1 The Aptitude of Holding Back

Strategic patience is a purposeful decision to wait it out while keeping an eye on and assessing the constantly changing power relations. It is not a passive condition of inaction. It calls for a thorough comprehension of the current circumstances, the parties involved, and the possible repercussions of acting too soon. When the timing is appropriate, one can position themselves to make a more significant move by practicing self-control and restraining themselves from acting impulsively.

9.2.2 The Observational Power

The smart influencer uses the skill of observation to glean important information while waiting for the right moment. It is possible to identify hidden patterns and predict future events by closely monitoring the interactions, motives, and actions of people in positions of authority. When it comes time to take action, the influencer can make better decisions because of their enhanced comprehension of the dynamics at play.

9.2.3 When it comes to timing, everything matters.

When it comes to subliminal influence, timing is a crucial component that can make or destroy a plan. Behaving too late can make one's efforts ineffective, while acting too soon might lead to lost chances or unexpected repercussions. An adept influencer must have the intuition and vision to sense when the power dynamic is most conducive to manipulation. This necessitates a thorough comprehension of the situation, the people involved, and the possible outcomes of one's actions.

9.2.4 The Skill of Forecasting

The capacity to foresee future developments and trends is another aspect of strategic patience. The influencer can put themselves in a position to seize new possibilities by closely examining the existing situation and forecasting possible outcomes. This calls for a blend of critical thinking, instinct, and in-depth knowledge of people's behavior. The patient influencer can even sway events before they happen by always being one step ahead of the game.

9.2.5 Impatience's Dangers
Although impatience can be a terrible trap, patience is a virtue. Hasty or impulsive decisions can have unforeseen consequences and reduce one's power. It is imperative to withstand the urge to act hastily without carefully weighing the benefits and hazards. In order to make sure that the time is appropriate and the intended result is attainable, the influencer must constantly balance the potential benefits against the potential costs.

9.2.6 The Timing Dance
Timing is a delicate dance that takes intuition and dexterity to master. It is an ability that can only be developed through practice and a thorough comprehension of power relations. The patient influencer needs to develop the ability to recognize the subliminal clues and signals that point to the ideal moments to act. This could entail taking advantage of outside happenings, cracking systems, or taking

advantage of changes in the balance of power. The influencer can optimize their impact and accomplish their desired results by carefully planning their activities.

9.2.7 The Rationale for Acting and Not Acting Being strategically patient does not mean being passive. Waiting for the perfect opportunity to act and acting decisively when the timing is right are two very different things. An adept influencer knows when to take action and when to wait, realizing that sometimes doing nothing at all is the most effective course of action. The influencer can keep control of the story and sway events in their favor by carefully calculating their actions.

9.2.8 The Extended Strategy Long-term thinking is often necessary for strategic patience. The influencer needs to be prepared to put in the time and energy necessary to develop rapport, create a foundation of trust, and construct the framework for further influence. This can entail giving up immediate benefits in favor of long-term achievement. The influencer who plays the long game might establish themselves as a reliable confidant or advisor and have access to opportunities and privileged knowledge that they would not otherwise have.

9.2.9 The Adaptation Art

Being patient is important, but you also need to be flexible and adaptive. The influencer needs to be ready to modify their plan when new opportunities and changing conditions present themselves. This necessitates a readiness to let go of assumptions and adopt novel strategies. The influencer may effectively negotiate the always-shifting power dynamics and maintain their influence by remaining adaptable and receptive to new ideas.

Strategic patience is a stitch that connects the several facets of power dynamics in the complex fabric of subtle impact. It's a skill that demands a careful balancing act between time, anticipation, and observation. The influencer can increase their impact and get the results they want by being skilled at waiting for the proper moment. We will go deeper into the skill of acting precisely and grasping opportunities in the upcoming chapter, which will broaden our comprehension of the dance of power.

9.3: Taking Advantage of Possibilities

Influence is fueled by opportunities. These are the times when everything comes together, and the way to success is obvious. Accurately taking advantage of these possibilities is essential to the art of subtle persuasion. It's the difference between making it big and failing, between stepping up the power ladder and staying in the background.

9.3.1 The Influence of Time

While dancing the influence dance, timing is crucial. It's the skill of timing your actions to best influence others, take action, and change the course of events. Seeing things clearly, comprehending the forces at work, and having the guts to move boldly when the timing is right are all necessary for seizing opportunities.

9.3.2 Interpreting the Indicators

In order to grasp opportunities, one needs to be aware of the subtle cues that point to a good time. These indicators may appear as a change in the balance of power, a shift in the situation, or even a vulnerable moment. You may recognize these cues and position yourself to benefit from them by paying close attention to the surroundings and the individuals involved.

9.3.3 Thoughtful Action

Taking advantage of opportunities requires planning rather than acting on impulse. It necessitates thorough planning, getting ready, and knowing exactly what you want to achieve. Behaving precisely entails analyzing the possible outcomes, balancing the risks, and making sure that your choices support your long-term objectives. It involves taking calculated risks to increase your chances of success and reduce the possibility of negative consequences.

9.3.4 Adaptability and Flexibility

Opportunities in the dance of influence can disappear at any time. They could emerge out of nowhere and vanish just as fast. You have to be nimble and adaptive to grab these opportunities. This entails being flexible enough to modify tactics, plans, and even goals as needed. It calls for quick thinking, the capacity to change course when things get complicated, and the ability to grab any new possibilities that come up.

9.3.5 The Will to Take Action

Taking the initiative is often necessary to seize chances. It entails coming out of hiding and into the open, confidently stating who you are and what you believe. It's about actively searching out chances rather than waiting for them to present themselves and being proactive as opposed to reactive. By taking the initiative, you can control the story, determine the course of events, and establish yourself as a major figure in the power struggles that are going on.

9.3.6 The Importance of Planning Effective opportunity seizing requires preparation. It entails obtaining data, assessing the circumstances, and creating a calculated action plan. You can foresee potential roadblocks and come up with solutions by being aware of the situation and the motivations of those involved. Developing your network, strengthening your abilities, and forming the partnerships required to bolster your influence are all aspects of preparation.

9.3.7 The Skill of Determining Danger Risk-taking is an intrinsic part of seizing chances. It necessitates pushing the envelope, standing up to the status quo, and possibly encountering pushback or opposition. Weighing the possible benefits against the potential costs is the art of risk assessment. It entails weighing the immediate and long-term effects of your choices and making defensible choices after carefully examining the circumstances.

9.3.8 Taking Lessons from Mistakes

Not every chance taken will result in achievement. A necessary component of the influence-seeking path is failure. Failure, though, should be viewed as a teaching moment rather than a setback. You can become stronger and more resilient by thinking back on your mistakes, figuring out what went wrong, and changing how you went about things. You can improve your chances of success and guide your future actions by learning important lessons from failure.

9.3.9 The Aspect of Ethics

Taking advantage of possibilities in the dance of influence brings up moral questions. It's critical to walk carefully on the boundary between manipulation and ethical influence. While taking advantage of chances may require strategic maneuvering, it is important to make sure that your activities are morally sound and do not injure other people. The goal of ethical influence is to establish win-win scenarios in which everyone wins and nobody is taken advantage of or duped.

9.3.10: The Sequence of Dances

The art of subtle influence involves a continuous practice of seizing opportunities. It calls for flexibility, unwavering attention to detail, and a profound comprehension of the power relationships at work. You can continue to take advantage of opportunities and influence the path of events by developing your abilities, improving your tactics, and remaining aware of how the world is changing. The art of grasping opportunities is an essential step on the lifelong journey that is the dance of influence.

9.4 Preventing Unintentional Repercussions and Backlash

One must constantly be aware of the possibility of blowbacks and unforeseen effects when engaging in the complex dance of subtle influence. Even though persuasive and manipulative skills can be quite powerful, it's important to proceed cautiously and with ethical considerations when using them. This chapter examines the significance of preventing backlash and unintended effects, offering readers advice and techniques to help them move gracefully and strategically through the shadow of influence.

9.4.1 The Ripple Effect: Recognizing Its Effects

Every influence has an effect, and every action has a response. It is critical to understand that influence activities, no matter how well-intentioned, can have unexpected consequences. We are changing the way people think, decide, and act when we manipulate or persuade them. This change has the potential to have far-reaching effects beyond what we originally intended.

It is crucial to think about the possible effects of our actions in order to prevent backlash and unforeseen repercussions. We need to consider how others could interpret our influence and how it might affect their lives. We may make better decisions and reduce the possibility of unfavorable outcomes by standing back and thinking about the bigger picture of what we do.

9.4.2 Unintentional Consequences Law According to the law of unintended consequences, our activities may have unanticipated repercussions that are frequently at odds with our initial goals. This law is especially important in the domain of influence. We must be mindful that our actions may have unforeseen consequences that could jeopardize our objectives or perhaps cause harm to others when we try to influence or persuade people.

Being humble and self-aware while approaching influence is essential to avoiding the law of unintended consequences. We have to acknowledge that unanticipated events can occur and that we do not always control how our actions turn out. By accepting this fact, we can reduce the likelihood of unfavorable outcomes by being better equipped to adapt and modify our plans as needed.

9.4.3 Ethical Issues: Juggling Authority and Obligation

It is crucial to keep a strong moral compass when pursuing influence. There is a huge deal of responsibility that comes with having influence over other people. We have to think about how our activities affect people individually and in society at large. Our judgments and actions should be guided by ethical principles to prevent injury or exploitation of others in our pursuit of power.

It is essential to create a balance between our individual objectives and the broader good in order to prevent backlash and unforeseen repercussions. We have to ask ourselves if the things we do are consistent with our ideals and make a good impact on the world. We can traverse the shadows of influence with integrity and reduce the possibility of unfavorable consequences by giving ethical issues first priority.

9.4.4 Strategic Thinking: Risk Prediction and Mitigation

Strategic thinking is essential to preventing backlash and unforeseen repercussions. It entails foreseeing possible dangers and creating backup strategies to lessen them. By being proactive, we may reduce the possibility of unfavorable results and better equip ourselves to deal with any obstacles that may arise.

A tactic to prevent retaliation is to carefully assess the possible responses of those we are trying to influence. We might modify our strategy to reduce resistance and increase receptiveness by placing ourselves in their position and learning about their viewpoints. Furthermore, by keeping the lines of communication open and aggressively seeking out feedback, we can recognize any unexpected repercussions early on and take appropriate action to rectify them.

Knowing the boundaries of our influence is a critical component of strategic thinking. We have to acknowledge that there are some things we cannot predict or control. By accepting this fact, we are able to concentrate on the things that we can control and use the knowledge at our disposal to make wise judgments.

9.4.5 Taking Lessons from Failures and Accepting Development and Adaptation Errors will inevitably occur along the path of impact, despite the best of intentions and strategic planning. It's critical to view circumstances involving blowback or unanticipated repercussions as chances for development and adaptability.

We may learn a lot about our own advantages and disadvantages as influences by thinking back on our decisions and the results of those decisions. We can modify our tactics and methods by taking the lessons we've learned from our errors. Adopting a growth mentality enables us to improve our abilities and become more adept at navigating influence's shadows.

9.4.6 Fostering Compassion and Empathy It is easy to lose sight of our own objectives and interests in the pursuit of influence. But it's crucial to develop empathy and compassion for other people in order to prevent retaliation and unforeseen repercussions. We can create more moral and practical tactics if we take into account the viewpoints and requirements of the people we are trying to influence.

Understanding others' feelings and motives through empathy enables us to adjust our strategy so that it appeals to them. Conversely, compassion makes sure that our acts are motivated by a sincere concern for other people's welfare. We may reduce the possibility of unfavorable outcomes and create stronger, more genuine relationships by bringing these traits into our encounters.

9.4.7 The Influence of Analysis and Introspection

Regular introspection and action analysis are essential to preventing retaliation and unforeseen repercussions. We may find any areas for improvement and make the required changes by taking the time to evaluate the results of our influence endeavors.

We can better comprehend our own reasons and the consequences of our acts when we reflect on them. It assists us in spotting trends and patterns that could have unforeseen repercussions. Evaluation, on the other hand, entails determining areas where we may improve our approach and objectively evaluating the efficacy of our efforts.

We can continuously learn and develop by adding reflection and evaluation to our influence practice. This will reduce the possibility of unfavorable outcomes and increase our capacity to move skillfully and morally through the shadows.

In   summary
One of the most important things about learning the art of subtle influence is avoiding backlash and unexpected repercussions. We can reduce the possibility of unfavorable outcomes by being aware of the possible knock-on implications of our decisions, thinking ethically, and using strategic thinking. Embracing change, developing compassion and understanding, and reflecting and evaluating on a regular basis all help us become more adept at navigating the shadows with grace and wisdom. Let us keep in mind the significance of preventing fallout and unforeseen consequences as we continue to delve into the depths of power dynamics and make sure that our influence is used in a morally and responsibly manner.

The Shadows of Resistance

10.1 Recognizing and Examining Opposition

One unavoidable factor that emerges while trying to influence someone is resistance. Understanding and dealing with resistance well is essential to getting desired results, whether in personal relationships, the workplace, or wider social contexts. This section will cover the different types of resistance, how to overcome them, how to gather allies and supporters, and how to modify our approach to get through this difficult situation.

10.1.1 The Character of Opposition Resistance can have many forms and be caused by a number of different things. To properly treat and overcome it, the fundamental causes must be found and examined. Here are a few typical examples of resistance:

Emotional Resistance: People who experience emotional resistance to change or to perceived threats to their values or interests are said to be exhibiting emotional resistance. It may show up as defensiveness, distrust, rage, or fear.

Intellectual Resistance: When people disagree with or contest the theories, justifications, or supporting data put out, intellectual resistance occurs. It could be the result of misunderstandings, conflicting viewpoints, or beliefs.

Structural Resistance: This type of resistance arises from the hierarchies, systems, and procedures that are in place and can make it difficult to adopt new ideas or bring about change. It may involve power relations, corporate policies, or bureaucratic red tape.

Cultural Resistance: When deeply rooted cultural norms, values, or traditions conflict with suggested modifications or ideas, cultural resistance is the result. Overcoming it can be difficult because it frequently entails questioning ingrained habits or beliefs.

Personal Resistance: Personal resistance stems from individual goals, objectives, or reasons that might not align with the intended results. It can be impacted by things like control desires, ego, and self-interest.

10.1.2 Techniques for Overcoming Opposition Resistance must be overcome with consideration and planning. Here are some tactics to think about:

Active listening and empathy: Make an effort to comprehend the worries, anxieties, or objections of people who are resisting. You can address their underlying needs and establish rapport by paying attention to what they have to say and showing empathy for their viewpoints.

Effective Communication: Create arguments that are compelling and that speak to the goals, values, and aspirations of the people who are resisting. Make sure your message is tailored to their particular issues and offers strong arguments for accepting change.

Education and Information: To dispel any misunderstandings, give precise and unambiguous information. Inform people of the advantages and possible advantages of the suggested modifications.

Collaboration and Inclusion: Ask those who are resisting to participate in the decision-making process and include them in it. You can lessen resistance and encourage a sense of ownership by involving them in the process.

Creating Coalitions and Allies: Find people or organizations that might support your cause or have similar objectives. You may strengthen your voice as a group and improve your chances of getting past opposition by forming partnerships.

Finding a common ground through compromise and negotiation can be useful in circumstances where opposition is firmly ingrained. By identifying win-win alternatives, you may resolve issues and proceed.

10.1.3 Creating Supporters and Allies
Constructing allies and followers is essential to breaking through opposition and gaining clout. Here are some tactics to think about:

Find Possible Allies: Look for people or organizations that might be receptive to your views or that have similar objectives. Seek out shared goals, values, or interests that could serve as the foundation of a cooperative partnership.

Develop Relationships: Take the time and make the effort to get to know possible allies. Talk to them in a meaningful way, give them your support, and show that you care about their   achievement.

Offer anything of value to prospective allies, such as knowledge, materials, or assistance. You may fortify the partnership and foster trust by exhibiting your desire to participate.

Work Together and Share Credit: Engage your allies in decision-making by working together and including them in the process. Give them credit for accomplishments and thank them for their help. This enhances the alliance and encourages a sense of ownership.

Keep Lines of Communication Open: Stay in constant contact with your allies, updating them on developments, difficulties, and chances. This guarantees that everyone is in agreement and able to modify tactics as necessary.

10.1.4 Modifying and Changing Strategies
It's critical to have an agile and flexible strategy while dealing with resistance. When changing your strategy, keep the following in mind:

Evaluate and Think: Keep evaluating the success of your plans and initiatives. Consider what is effective and what requires modification. Learn from your mistakes and triumphs, and be receptive to criticism.

It takes time to overcome barriers, so have

patience. Be tenacious and patient in your endeavors. Understand that things might not materialize right away, and be ready to modify your expectations and schedule accordingly.

Get Input: Consistently ask people you are attempting to persuade for their input. Recognize their viewpoints and apply their knowledge to improve your strategy. This shows that you're willing to pay attention and change.

Try New Things and Innovate: Show an open mind to attempting novel strategies and varying your approach. Innovation can assist in overcoming obstacles and revealing fresh avenues for influence.

You may navigate the shadows of resistance and improve your odds of reaching your intended outcomes by recognizing and evaluating opposition, using effective techniques, forming alliances, and modifying tactics. Recall that mastering this power dance necessitates both resilience and dexterity, and that comprehending resistance is a critical first step.

10.2   Techniques   for   Overcoming Opposition

Resistance is an inevitable impediment in the complex dance of subtle influence that one must learn to overcome. Resistance can be a serious obstacle to anyone trying to exercise their influence, regardless of its source—personal prejudices, competing interests, or a fear of change. However, you may overcome resistance and accomplish your goals if you have the correct tactics and a thorough understanding of human psychology. In this section, we'll look at some practical methods for getting over opposition and persuading even the most doubtful people.

10.2.1 Recognizing the Origin of Opposition It's important to identify the cause of resistance before attempting to overcome it. There are many other reasons why people resist, including fear, mistrust, or feeling as though their interests or beliefs are in danger. You may modify your strategy and attend to the particular issues raised by the resistant party by determining the underlying reasons for their opposition.

10.2.2 Establishing rapport and trust

Developing rapport and trust with those concerned is one of the most effective ways to overcome resistance. Without trust, efforts to overcome opposition are likely to be ineffective, since trust is the cornerstone around which influence is constructed. Make the effort to connect with them on a sincere level, pay attention to their worries, and show empathy. You can start to close the distance and foster mutual understanding by demonstrating your comprehension and respect for their viewpoint.

10.2.3 Presenting the Content

Your message's framing can have a big impact on how people understand and interpret it. It is crucial to present your arguments in a way that is consistent with the values and goals of the person who is resisting. You can make your ideas seem more appealing by emphasizing the potential advantages and addressing any potential disadvantages. A sense of common purpose can also be established, and early suspicion can be dispelled by speaking in a way that is consistent with the values and beliefs of the opposing party.

10.2.4 Presenting Proof and Establishing Credibility

Lack of faith or confidence in the person or concept being offered is frequently the root cause of resistance. In order to go past this, you must prove your credibility and offer proof. You can accomplish this by offering evidence to back up your arguments, such as case studies, data, or testimonies. Highlighting your knowledge, experience, or successful track record can also help you project credibility and allay any concerns.

10.2.5 Seeking Mutual Understanding

One effective tactic for getting beyond resistance is to find areas of agreement with the other side. Establishing common objectives, principles, or passions can foster cohesion and cooperation. Highlight the areas where your goals coincide and give an example of how your suggested solution can contribute to the attainment of shared gains. You can boost the likelihood of receiving support from the reluctant party by appealing to their self-interest and presenting your ideas as a win-win scenario.

10.2.6 Resolving Issues and Reluctance

Real worries or objections are frequently the source of resistance. Directly addressing these concerns is crucial, as opposed to brushing them off or disregarding them. Spend some time actively listening to them so you can comprehend the underlying causes of their concerns. After you've determined what worries them, give them well-considered, reassuring answers that allay their worries and show that you've given them careful attention.

10.2.7 Forming Alliances and Coalitions
When resistance is faced alone, it might be difficult to overcome. Creating alliances and coalitions can greatly improve your position and raise your chances of success. Seek the assistance of people or organizations who share your goals or who have sway over the opposition. Using the strength of group influence, you can put up a united front that will have a higher chance of overcoming obstacles and achieving your goals.

10.2.8 Sturdiness and Flexibility
Adaptability and perseverance are frequently needed to overcome barriers. Understanding that change takes time and that initial resistance does not always indicate failure is crucial. Be tenacious and patient in your endeavors, continuously evaluating your strategy and making adjustments as needed.

Over time, you can improve your tactics and raise your odds of conquering resistance by staying adaptable and receptive to criticism.

Overcoming opposition in the complex dance of subtle influence is a skill that may be developed and perfected. You can navigate the shadows of resistance and accomplish your desired outcomes by understanding the source of resistance, developing rapport and trust, framing your message effectively, supplying evidence and establishing your credibility, identifying common ground, addressing concerns and objections, forming coalitions and allies, and remaining persistent and adaptable. Recall that the art of subtle influence is about knowing others and convincing them of the worth of your ideas, not about dominating them.

10.3: Creating Supporters and Allies
The creation of allies and followers is an essential stage in accomplishing your objectives in the complex dance of power. Even though the art of subtle influence frequently entails working behind the scenes, it is crucial to build connections and relationships with people who can further your goals. This chapter delves into tactics and methods for forming partnerships and winning people over, so that your influence grows beyond your own talents.

10.3.1 Finding Possible Allies
Finding people who can share your goals is crucial before you start the process of cultivating allies and supporters. Seek out individuals with comparable objectives, principles, or passions. Take into account their networks, skills, and positions of power. These people can turn into important allies in your pursuit of subliminal influence.

To spot possible allies, watch how they behave, listen to what they have to say, and watch how they connect with other people. Seek out indications of agreement, like similar viewpoints, adversaries, or goals. It is imperative to take into account the power and influence dynamics inherent in the particular setting in which you find yourself operating. Determine the influential people and power brokers who have the most influence over your capacity to succeed.

10.3.2 Fostering Connections Building ties with possible allies is the next step after identifying them. For partnerships to last, sincere connections founded on mutual respect, trust, and benefit are necessary. Here are some tactics to think about:

10.3.2.1 Developing a Relationship Building rapport is the cornerstone of any fruitful partnership. Seek areas of agreement with prospective allies and have deep discussions with them. Express sincere curiosity about their viewpoints, backgrounds, and objectives. You may establish a rapport and provide the foundation for future cooperation by exhibiting empathy and comprehension.

10.3.2.2 Offering Support: Assisting prospective allies is a useful strategy for forming alliances. Determine their requirements, obstacles, or goals, and come up with solutions to help them. This could be lending out resources, giving counsel, or donating your knowledge. By displaying your readiness to assist, you position yourself as a beneficial and trustworthy partner.

10.3.2.3 Establishing trust is an essential component of any connection, but it's particularly important when forging partnerships. Keep your word when you say it, honor your agreements, and keep information private when it's required. Since trust must be gained over time, it is critical to constantly show your dependability and honesty.

10.3.2.4 Linked In Forging relationships and obtaining support need networking. Attend pertinent conferences, parties, or events to network with possible allies. Talk to each other, share ideas, and build relationships. Engage in active participation in professional or social networks to broaden your horizons and boost the likelihood of discovering like-minded people who can assist you in your pursuits.

10.3.3 Teamwork Techniques Collaboration is often necessary to forge coalitions and win support. You may foster a sense of ownership and involvement in your objectives by asking others to participate in your decision-making process and provide their opinions. Here are some tactics to think about:

10.3.3.1 Requesting Feedback and Input
Invite prospective allies to participate in the decision-making process by asking for their opinions and suggestions. This encourages a sense of ownership and cooperation, in addition to showing respect for their area of expertise. You will be more likely to win their support if you respect their perspectives.

10.3.3.2 Developing Win-Win Circumstances
Establishing win-win scenarios where both sides gain is crucial when forming partnerships. Determine the ways in which your objectives coincide with those of your possible allies and come up with win-win solutions. You will be more likely to win their support if you can show them that your goals are not only selfish.

10.3.3.3 Team-Based Initiatives
Building relationships and gaining support is a great opportunity that collaborative ventures offer. You develop a sense of camaraderie and shared purpose when you collaborate to achieve a common objective. Working on

collaborative projects also gives you the chance to demonstrate your abilities, knowledge, and dedication to prospective allies.

10.3.4 Sustaining and Developing Partnerships

Forming coalitions is a continual process that needs constant work and attention; it is not a one-time event. It is vital to uphold and cultivate the relationships you have formed once you have secured the support of others. Here are some tactics to think about:

10.3.4.1 Interaction and Cooperation

Keep the lines of communication open with your partners and allies. Provide them with regular updates on your work, solicit their opinions, and, when appropriate, include them in decision-making processes. Partnerships are strengthened by cooperation and constant communication, which also keep your allies interested and on your side.

10.3.4.2 Mutual Aid

One effective strategy for preserving coalitions is reciprocity. Be prepared to give your supporters the same support and help that you have received. Seek out chances to assist people in overcoming obstacles or achieving their objectives. By exhibiting your dedication to their accomplishments, you bolster the reciprocal advantages of your partnership.

10.3.4.3 Dispute Settlement
In any relationship, disagreements and conflicts are unavoidable. When disagreements emerge within your coalitions, resolve them quickly and amicably. Make an effort to comprehend the viewpoints of all parties concerned and endeavor to arrive at solutions that satisfy each of you. Resolving conflicts well guarantees the life of your partnerships and improves relationships.

Gaining friends and supporters is essential to being skilled at the art of subliminal influence. You can develop connections, find possible allies, and use cooperative strategies to broaden your area of influence and improve your chances of success. Recall that forming alliances takes time, work, and sincere dedication. Keep your channels of communication open, nurture your relationships, and show a willingness to help others in return. You may move through the shadows of opposition and over hurdles on your way to subtle influence when you have a network of pals by your side.

10.4 Modifying and Adapting Strategies

In the complex dance of subliminal influence, flexibility and adaptation are essential. Realize that no two situations are the same as you negotiate the shadows of resistance. What could have been beneficial in one situation might not be in another. In order to become a true expert in subtle influence, one must be flexible enough to modify strategies to fit the shifting dynamics of power.

10.4.1 Accepting Adaptability

In the domain of influence, inflexibility is detrimental. Success depends on one's capacity for adaptation and strategy modification. A master of subtle influence must be sensitive to the subtleties of every circumstance, much as a skilled dancer adapts their moves to the beat of the music. This necessitates a thorough comprehension of the parties involved, the environment in which influence is being used, and the intended result.

10.4.2 Evaluating the Circumstance

Evaluating the current circumstances is essential before making any changes to your strategy. Spend time learning about the situation, observing the dynamics at work, and examining the underlying motives and aspirations of the individuals engaged. This will offer insightful information about the most effective course of action. Recall that resistance can manifest itself in a variety of ways, and the first step in conquering them is realizing the particular challenges you confront.

10.4.3 Communication Flexibility
Subtle influence is largely dependent on communication, and when you encounter opposition, you must modify your approach. Different people react differently to different strategies, so what works for one person might not work for another. You may improve the likelihood that your message will be heard and comprehended by making changes to your language, tone, and delivery. To customize your message to the unique requirements and preferences of your audience, you must be able to read between the lines and engage in active listening.

10.4.4 Making Use of Supporters and Allies
It helps to keep in mind that you are not alone when facing resistance. Creating allies and a network of support can help you handle challenges far more effectively. These

supporters may give insightful opinions, present different viewpoints, and even amplify your cause. You can use the network's combined strength to overcome obstacles by modifying your strategy to incorporate cooperation and teamwork.

10.4.5   Tenacity   and   Waiting
Patience and persistence are needed while changing and refining strategies. It is normal to have obstacles along the rarely straight path to influence. But you can weather the storms of resistance and keep moving forward if you stay patient and unwavering in your desire. Keep in mind that gaining influence is a long-term game, and people who can adapt and modify their strategies over time frequently succeed.

10.4.6 Taking Lessons from Mistakes
The path to becoming an expert in the art of subtle persuasion will inevitably include failure. When faced with resistance, it's critical to see failures as chances for development and education. Give yourself some time to consider what went wrong, evaluate your strategy, and pinpoint areas that need work. As a teacher, you can improve your strategies and raise your chances of success in subsequent undertakings by accepting failure.

10.4.7 Harmonizing Sturdiness and Adaptability

It takes a careful dance to strike the right balance between tenacity and adaptability. As crucial as it is to stick to your course of action, it's also critical to know when a shift in strategy is required. This calls for a thorough comprehension of the circumstances, the parties involved, and the intended result. You can modify and tweak your strategies while adhering to your main goals by regularly evaluating and reevaluating your approach.

10.4.8 Adopting Ethical Principles

It's critical to keep ethical issues in mind as you modify and refine your strategies. Although it can be easy to act dishonestly and with disregard for others, it is crucial to always conduct yourself honorably. Aim to achieve a balance between following moral ideals and accomplishing your aims. You can handle the complexity of power dynamics with grace and truthfulness if you do this.

Success in the dynamic world of power dynamics requires flexibility and adaptability. You can gracefully move through the shadows of opposition by accepting fluidity, evaluating the circumstances, modifying your communication approach, enlisting supporters, and remaining persistent and patient. Never forget to act morally at all times, balance tenacity and adaptability, and learn from your mistakes. By doing this, you will develop into an expert in the subtle influence technique, able to modify your strategies in order to get the results you want.

The Dance of Influence in the Digital Age

11.1 The Influence of Online and Social Media Platforms

The emergence of social media and online platforms has led to an exponential expansion of the landscape of influence in the current digital age. These platforms have developed into effective tools that let people and organizations interact, communicate, and have an impact on the world stage. Social media's power comes from its instantaneous ability to reach large audiences across traditional borders and geographic locations. To become an expert at the art of subtle influence, one must thus comprehend and utilize the power of social media and online platforms.

Social media's ascent
Social networking sites like LinkedIn, Instagram, Twitter, Facebook, and Twitter have completely changed how individuals communicate and exchange information. These platforms have developed into online communities where people can interact, express themselves, and have discussions. With the emergence of social media, people may now share their ideas, opinions, and thoughts with a worldwide audience, democratizing the flow of information.

Increasing Impact
People have a special chance to expand their audience and increase their impact through social media. A single tweet or post has the ability to reach millions of people, which makes social media an effective instrument

for community mobilization, idea dissemination, and public opinion formation. Social media is a powerful tool for organizing movements, bringing attention to social concerns, and pushing for change since it allows users to interact with like-minded people and create online communities.

Impact   Culture
A new generation of online celebrities that have gained substantial followings and influence has emerged as a result of influencer culture, in addition to the power of social media as a platform for individuals. Influencers have the power to alter customer behavior, advertise goods and services, and impact prevailing trends. They are frequently subject matter experts or fanatics in particular subjects. Their followers take their recommendations and endorsements seriously, which makes them an invaluable resource for marketers and brands.

Getting Around in Online Communities
It is essential to comprehend the characteristics of online communities in order to traverse the world of social media and online platforms efficiently. Understanding the subtleties of each platform's culture, customs, and etiquette is crucial to effectively

interacting with the audience. It takes constant involvement, active participation, and flexibility to adjust to the ever-changing digital scene in order to have a great online presence.

Using social media to gain influence Creating a strategy plan is essential to leveraging the subtly influential power of social media and internet platforms. Here are some crucial things to remember:

Determine who your intended audience is. Recognize the people you wish to impact and develop content that speaks to their goals, values, and areas of interest.

Produce engaging content: Write shareable, educational, and amusing content. Utilize multimedia, images, and storytelling strategies to draw in and hold the interest of your audience.

Develop a powerful personal brand by continuously offering insightful commentary, in-depth knowledge, and original viewpoints. This will position you as an authority in your industry. Develop a powerful web presence that speaks to your target audience and embodies your beliefs.

Interact with the people in your audience: engage in dialogue, reply to messages and comments, and cultivate deep relationships with your fans. Express sincere curiosity about their thoughts and suggestions.

Work together with influencers: Find influential people in your field or sector and see if you can work together. A larger audience can be reached, and your message can be amplified by collaborating with influencers.

Track and evaluate results: Keep a close eye on the outcomes of your social media initiatives. Utilize analytics tools to learn more about the demographics of your audience, engagement metrics, and the success of your content strategy. Utilize the data to modify your strategy in order to maximize your impact.

The Negative Aspects of Digital Impact Online platforms and social media present a wealth of influence opportunities, but they also carry certain risks and ethical issues. Some of the darker sides of digital influence include the ease with which false information can be disseminated, the frequency of online harassment, and the ability to manipulate public opinion. It's critical to handle internet influence with accountability, integrity, and a dedication to moral behavior.

Digital Realm Ethics: A Critical Review

It is imperative that those who aspire to become experts in the art of nuanced influence navigate the digital sphere with morality in mind. Here are some essential values to follow:

Honesty and openness: Be open and honest about your goals, connections, and any possible conflicts of interest. Be truthful in all of your communications, and refrain from using dishonest or fraudulent tactics.

Empathy and respect: In both online and offline interactions, show others these qualities. Steer clear of any destructive activity, including cyberbullying and online harassment.

Integrity and accuracy: Make sure the material you offer is accurate, and work to add value for your audience. Make sure your content is fact-checked, and refrain from using clickbait or disseminating false information.

Privacy and consent: Be considerate of others' privacy and permission. Prior to releasing any personal information or photos, get consent and consider the possible repercussions of your conduct.

Accountability and accountability: Own up to the consequences of your influence and your internet presence. Take responsibility for your words and deeds, and keep an open mind to suggestions and helpful criticism.

People can use social media and online platforms to constructively affect others and navigate the digital sphere with integrity by adhering to these ethical guidelines.

In conclusion, it is important to recognize the influence that social media and internet platforms have in the digital age. These platforms have completely changed how people interact, communicate, and wield power. Mastering the art of subtle influence requires knowing how to navigate online communities, capitalize on influencer culture, and comprehend the intricacies of social media dynamics. But it's crucial to approach digital influence with ethical considerations in mind, making sure that all online interactions are genuine, transparent, respectful, and accountable. People can increase their influence and have a positive digital impact by using social media in an ethical manner.

11.2 Getting Around Influencer Culture and Online Communities

The sphere of influence has greatly broadened in the digital age. Social media and online communities have developed into effective instruments that people and groups can use to alter public opinion, impact public sentiment, and subtly affect global affairs. A thorough grasp of the dynamics at work and the capacity to modify conventional tactics to take advantage of the special opportunities and difficulties that the digital sphere presents are necessary for navigating this new landscape.

11.2.1 The Development of Virtual Communities

Like-minded people get together in online communities to exchange thoughts, opinions, and life experiences, and these groups have grown into thriving centers of social interaction. These communities are present on a number of platforms, including specialist websites, social media groups, and forums. Since people may interact with others who share their interests and values, they offer a fertile field for influence and foster a sense of camaraderie and belonging.

Understanding the dynamics of online communities is necessary for good navigation. Every group has its own customs, laws, and hierarchies of authority. Because they are regarded as authorities or experts in their industries, influencers within these groups have a great deal of influence over their members. People can progressively increase their own influence in the community by interacting with these influencers and offering insightful commentary.

11.2.2 The Influencer Culture's Power
The internet world now prominently features influencer culture. Influencers are people who have a sizable social media following, frequently as a result of their knowledge, charm, or distinctive viewpoints. They have the power to sway beliefs, advertise goods and services, and even spark societal change.

Understanding the nuances of these people's motivations and tactics is essential for navigating influencer culture. Influencers frequently develop a personal brand that reflects the passions and goals of their target audience. In addition to using their power to forge alliances and partnerships with companies, they meticulously select their content to uphold authenticity and trustworthiness.

Finding and interacting with influencers who have similar values and interests is crucial for anyone looking to subtly impact the influencer culture. Through sincere connections, people can use these influencers' platforms to magnify and reach a wider audience with their own thoughts.

11.2.3 Establishing Real Connections Creating genuine ties is essential to influencing subtly in the digital sphere. Sincere participation and deep connections are essential to the health of online communities and influencer cultures. Skepticism and opposition are sometimes encountered with flimsy techniques or overt self-promotion.

It takes time and effort to establish genuine connections in order to successfully navigate influencer culture and online communities. This entails engaging in dialogue, offering insightful commentary, and exhibiting a sincere interest in the community's or influencer's content. People can progressively acquire influence and subtly and meaningfully impact opinions by making a name for themselves as reliable and respected members of the community.

11.2.4 Making the Most of Social Media Social media platforms have completely changed how people and organizations interact and wield power. These platforms offer a wide range of features and tools that can be used to successfully traverse the digital environment.

People who want to successfully use social media platforms need to be aware of the distinctive characteristics of each platform. Various platforms have their own set of guidelines and best practices in addition to serving diverse audiences. Users can increase their effect and reach by customizing their strategy for each platform.

People also need to keep up with the constantly changing trends and algorithms that influence social media sites. People may optimize their tactics to make sure their messages are viewed by the correct audience at the right time by knowing how material is prioritized and promoted.

11.2.5 Online Influence's Drawbacks Online communities and influencer culture provide enormous potential for subtly influencing others, but they also bring special difficulties and moral dilemmas. The internet is full of fake news, echo chambers, and manipulation opportunities.

People need to exercise caution when navigating these traps to make sure their influence is used in an ethical and responsible manner. It is crucial to assess information critically, verify the accuracy of sources, and encourage genuineness and openness. People may navigate online communities and influencer culture in a way that promotes positive change and real connections by upholding integrity and ethical standards.

To sum up, successfully navigating influencer culture and online communities demands both a thorough comprehension of the dynamics at work and the capacity to modify conventional tactics for use in digital environments. People may skillfully navigate this new terrain and subtly affect the digital age by creating genuine connections, utilizing social media platforms, and remaining aware of the risks and ethical issues.

11.3 The Negative Aspects of Digital Impact

Today's connected and technologically advanced world has made the digital sphere an effective instrument for persuasion and influence. The way we engage, communicate, and sway public opinion has changed dramatically as a result of social media platforms, online communities, and influencer culture. But this newfound power has a negative side that needs to be recognized and comprehended.

11.3.1 The Intumescence of Deception A new generation of influencers, capable of influencing public opinion, crafting narratives, and controlling large crowds, has emerged as a result of the digital era. These digital manipulators may have a big impact on people and communities by using well-crafted messages, deliberate targeting, and psychological weaknesses.

The ease with which disinformation may proliferate online is one of the most worrying features of digital influence. Propaganda, conspiracy theories, and false narratives can take off swiftly and sway public opinion. The speed and scope of digital platforms make it difficult to discern between reality and fiction, which erodes confidence in more established sources of information.

11.3.2 The Usage of Social Media as a Weapon

Once heralded as instruments for communication and connection, social media platforms have evolved into arenas for manipulation and power struggles. These platforms' algorithms, which prioritize sensationalist content and reinforce preexisting opinions, are made to promote interaction. This further polarizes society and makes it simpler for manipulators to take advantage of preexisting divisions by creating echo chambers where people are exposed to a narrow variety of viewpoints.

The anonymity that the internet provides also makes it easier for harassment, hate speech, and cyberbullying to proliferate. Online trolls and mobs have the ability to injure people and organizations severely and ruin reputations. Online abuse can have a catastrophic psychological impact, increasing the risk of anxiety, sadness, and even suicide.

11.3.3 Data Exploitation and Privacy

The emergence of digital technology has also given rise to worries about data abuse and privacy. Large volumes of personal data are gathered on people by businesses and organizations, frequently without their knowledge or consent. After then, this information is utilized to target specific people with tailored advertisements, change their behavior, and affect how they make decisions.

The Cambridge Analytica controversy brought to light the potential risks associated with data exploitation, as it involved the collection of personal information belonging to millions of Facebook users and its use for political purposes. The incident called into question the morality of data collection as well as the need for increased openness and regulation in the digital domain.

11.3.4 The Deception of Genuineness Authenticity is a highly prized asset in the age of digital influence. Genuine and relatable influencers have the power to gain enormous followings and exert a great deal of power. On the other hand, the quest for authenticity is frequently a skillfully constructed delusion.

A lot of influencers design their online personas with great care, showcasing a highly polished version of themselves that might not be entirely accurate. A group of experts may be working behind the scenes to plan each post, edit photos, and write material. This carefully calibrated genuineness may lead to inflated hopes as well as low self-esteem and feelings of inadequacy in followers.

11.3.5 Preventing Cyber-Manipulation

It is critical for people navigating the digital landscape to be conscious of the negative aspects of digital influence and to take precautions against manipulation. Here are some tactics to think about:

Critical Thinking: Learn how to assess sources and information critically. Examine the motivations underlying communications and take into account different viewpoints.

Media literacy: Become knowledgeable about digital and media literacy. Learn how information circulates, how algorithms operate, and how to spot false information.

Privacy Protection: Take precautions to keep your online privacy safe. Pay attention to the data you disclose and check the privacy settings on social networking sites.

Diverse Perspectives: Talk to people who have various opinions and look for a variety of information sources. This can assist in preventing the echo chamber effect and encourage a more impartial comprehension of difficult problems.

Fact-checking: Confirm facts before disseminating them. Websites that verify information might be useful in spotting inaccurate or deceptive content.

Build emotional fortitude to tolerate harassment and abuse on the internet. If necessary, ask friends, family, or mental health specialists for assistance.

Ethical Participation: Exercise caution in your own online conduct. Respect and kindness should be shown to others, and negative behavior should not be participated in or encouraged.

We can traverse the digital sphere with better awareness and safeguard ourselves from its possible damages by comprehending the dark side of digital influence and taking proactive measures to guard against manipulation. Positive change can be achieved through leveraging the power of digital influence, but maintaining ethical standards in our online interactions and being watchful at all times are essential.

11.4 Digital Realm Ethical Considerations
Ethical considerations become crucial in the digital age, as information is easily accessible and influence can be exerted with a single click. It is imperative that we consider the moral ramifications of our acts and the possible effects they may have on people and society at large as we traverse the enormous terrain of the internet world. This chapter delves into the ethical dilemmas that emerge in the context of digital influence, illuminating our shared responsibility in the dance of subliminal influence.

11.4.1 Digital Influence: Its Power and Responsibilities
The ability to influence people is now more accessible than ever, thanks to social media and online platforms. With only one post or tweet, anybody may now influence public opinion and reach large audiences. But there's a big responsibility that goes along with this increased authority. Understanding the possible effects that our words and deeds may have on other people is crucial, as is making ethical and responsible use of our influence.

11.4.2 Sincerity and Openness

Authenticity and transparency are essential ethical factors in the digital sphere. It is our duty as influencers to communicate with people in a sincere and truthful manner. This entails being open and honest about our goals, declaring any conflicts of interest, and refraining from dishonest tactics that could mislead or manipulate our audience. We can establish credibility and trust by remaining genuine and open, which will help us create deep connections with the people we want to impact.

11.4.3 Confidentiality and Assent

Respecting other people's consent and privacy is another essential ethical factor in the digital sphere. It's critical to have the required consent and treat personal data carefully when we collect data and communicate online. In addition to being required by law, upholding people's right to privacy and guaranteeing the protection of their personal data is also morally right.

11.4.4 Juggling self-interest with the common good

Achieving digital influence requires finding a balance between one's own interests and those of society at large. Seeking achievement and recognition is normal, but we must also be mindful of the possible effects our actions may have on other people and society at large. Digital influencers that are ethical see the value of leveraging their platform to support disadvantaged voices, encourage positive change, and enhance the online community.

11.4.5 Eliminating False and Misinformation
It is the duty of moral digital influencers to dispel lies and advance truth in an age of fake news and widespread disinformation. We can stop the spread of false information and promote an informed and educated online community by fact-checking and confirming the information we share. In order to enable their audience to separate fact from fiction, ethical digital influencers also work to advance media literacy and critical thinking.

11.4.6 Having Fruitful Conversations
The internet may frequently serve as a fertile environment for animosity and division. Digital influencers that uphold ethics recognize the value of polite discourse and constructive engagement. Through the cultivation of empathy, comprehension, and receptiveness, they establish forums for the exchange of varied viewpoints and thought-provoking

conversations. In addition to actively combating cyberbullying and harassment, ethical digital influencers also aim to make the internet a safer and more welcoming place.

11.4.7 Steer clear of exploitation and manipulation.
It's critical to steer clear of exploitation and manipulative strategies when pursuing influence. Digital influencers that uphold ethics are aware of the power dynamics at work and make a conscious effort to utilize their influence in a way that does not involve preying on the weak or abusing their audience. They put other people's liberty and well-being first, making sure that everything they do is morally right and doesn't hurt anyone.

11.4.8 Responsibility and Accountability
Ultimately, moral digital influencers accept accountability and own up to their mistakes. They are ready to receive criticism and grow from their errors because they understand that the things they say and do have an impact. They contribute to a culture of ethical digital influence and set an example for others by being accountable to themselves.

In conclusion, when it comes to ethical issues in the art of subtle persuasion, the digital environment offers both opportunities and obstacles. It is crucial to consider the authority and accountability that come with digital influence as we navigate this constantly changing environment. An online community where the dance of influence is governed by moral principles can be shaped by ethical digital influencers who prioritize authenticity, transparency, privacy, and the greater good.

Mastering the Dance

12.1 Power in Individual Connections
Our lives rest on our personal relationships. They influence our feelings, experiences, and general wellbeing. Complex and multifaceted are the dynamics of human connections, be they with family, friends, or love partners. We will examine how to improve and manage

these connections by using the concepts of subtle influence in this chapter.

12.1.1 Establishing rapport and trust

The foundations of any good relationship are rapport and trust. Building great trust and rapport is essential to using subtle influence in personal relationships. Empathy, active listening, and sincere interest in the thoughts and feelings of the other person are ways to do this.

In addition to hearing what is being said, active listening entails observing nonverbal clues and underlying emotions. You foster an atmosphere of openness and trust by exhibiting your complete presence and engagement in the discussion. This promotes a deeper connection by giving the other person a sense of being heard and understood.

Another crucial component of developing rapport and trust is empathy. You can build a closer relationship by seeing yourself in their position and appreciating their viewpoint. By being empathetic, you affirm their feelings and experiences and establish a secure environment in which candid dialogue is encouraged.

Sincere curiosity about the feelings and thoughts of the other person is an effective way to establish rapport. You can show that you respect their ideas and experiences by posing meaningful questions and making an effort to learn about their passions and interests. This establishes mutual respect and a sense of connectedness, which prepares the basis for subtle influence.

12.1.2 Recognizing Needs and Motivations In order to subtly impact interpersonal interactions, one must be aware of the needs and motives of those involved. Every individual has a distinct set of goals, anxieties, and desires that influence their choices and behaviors. Understanding these underlying motives can help you modify your strategy to suit their requirements and objectives.

Gaining insight into the intentions of others is largely dependent on observation and attentive listening. You may learn a lot about someone's desires and concerns by observing their words, body language, and behaviors. With this understanding, you can structure your conversations so that they align with their goals and improve the chances of a successful outcome.

But it's crucial to approach this comprehension with respect and sensitivity. It is never acceptable to employ subtle influence to control or take advantage of someone for one's own benefit. Rather, it ought to be utilized to promote understanding, cooperation, and relationship development between the parties.

12.1.3 Powerful Interaction and Settlement of Disputes

Relationships require communication to survive. It is essential to become skilled in good communication if you want to establish subtle influence. This entails actively listening to the other person's viewpoint in addition to openly expressing your own thoughts and feelings.

Creating messages that are convincing is a crucial component of good communication. You can make the other person more open to your influence by carefully selecting your words and phrasing your ideas in a way that aligns with their values and beliefs. Nonetheless, honesty can undermine trust and harm a relationship, so it's critical to communicate in a true and authentic manner.

Any relationship will inevitably experience conflict. It's critical to approach disagreements with a collaborative and compromise-focused perspective. You may resolve disagreements in a way that keeps the connection intact and fortifies your link with the other person by looking for areas of agreement and coming up with solutions that will benefit both parties.

12.1.4 Maintaining and Strengthening Bonds Subtle influence is a continuous process rather than an isolated occurrence. Maintaining a personal relationship requires time and work on your part in order to grow and thrive. This can be achieved through consistent communication, deeds of kindness, and exhibiting sincere concern and care for the other person.

Maintaining open lines of communication is essential to the relationship's survival. Regular communication, whether by phone conversations, texts, or in-person meetings, demonstrates your appreciation for the relationship and your commitment to its development.

Kindness has a powerful effect on fostering interpersonal relationships. Small acts of kindness that build a positive emotional connection, like supporting, expressing gratitude, or pleasantly surprising someone with a thoughtful present, can go a long way.

Maintaining personal relationships requires genuinely showing concern and caring for the other person. You build mutual trust and support by taking an active interest in their life, being there for them at difficult times, and recognizing and applauding their accomplishments.

In summary, the skill of subtle influence can be used in interpersonal interactions to promote mutual development, increase understanding, and establish trust. Through the use of nurturing actions, good communication, empathy, and active listening, you may skillfully and gracefully negotiate the complexity of intimate relationships. Recall that the purpose of subtle influence in interpersonal interactions is to foster a fulfilling and harmonious bond built on respect and understanding rather than to manipulate or control.

12.2 Inconspicuous Impact at Work

The workplace is a special place where people from different backgrounds come together to accomplish shared objectives. The skill of subtly influencing others is vital in this dynamic environment for managing power relationships, forming alliances, and succeeding both personally and professionally. The nuances of subtle influence in the workplace will be discussed in this chapter, along with methods, approaches, and moral concerns that might assist people in becoming adept at the dance of power.

12.2.1 Comprehending Power Dynamics and Organizational Culture

Understanding the underlying corporate culture and power relations is crucial before exploring the world of subtle influence in the workplace. Every company has a distinct set of standards, customs, and beliefs that influence how its employees behave and interact with one another. Understanding the culture of the organization helps people recognize the sources of influence and power in the workplace hierarchy.

Formal authority, knowledge, and social ties are just a few examples of the different ways that power dynamics inside an organization can manifest. By identifying key stakeholders and power brokers who can help them achieve their objectives, people can strategically navigate the organizational environment by understanding these power dynamics.

12.2.2 Influencing Up: Techniques for Winning the Support of Superiors
It might be difficult and delicate to influence superiors. Nonetheless, people might win the respect and approval of their superiors by using subtle influence tactics. Aligning one's objectives with those of the company and presenting concepts and ideas in a way that emphasizes their potential advantages for the company as a whole are two effective strategies.

Gaining the support of superiors also requires developing a connection and earning their trust. Through attentively hearing their worries, comprehending their viewpoints, and exhibiting a sincere desire for their prosperity, people can cultivate favorable connections that pave the way for impact.

12.2.3 Creating Alliances and Managing Peers
Peers can be competitors as well as allies on

the job. Maintaining relationships with peers means striking a careful balance between cooperation and rivalry. Building a reputation for competence, fairness, and honesty helps people form alliances and become important members of teams.

In order to manage relationships with peers, effective communication is essential. People can build strong relationships and have an impact on their peers by actively listening, empathizing, and establishing common ground. Building alliances requires cooperation and collaboration because it allows people to take advantage of the group's aggregate power to accomplish common goals.

12.2.4 Taking the Lead from the Shadows: Managing Underlings

Effective leadership involves more than just imposing one's will on others; it also involves motivating and influencing followers. When it comes to leading from the shadows, subtle influence tactics can be especially useful since they let leaders mentor and inspire their group members without resorting to overt displays of authority.

Knowing the demands and motives of your subordinates is a crucial part of influencing them. Leaders may cultivate an environment that promotes productivity, engagement, and loyalty by acknowledging and resolving these concerns. Setting realistic goals, giving encouragement and acknowledgment, and giving clear instructions are all effective ways to persuade subordinates.

12.2.5 Office Politics: The Craft of Persuasion Although office politics can be a difficult environment to navigate, it can also be a place where subtle influence can flourish. One can effectively navigate office politics and exercise influence by having a thorough understanding of the unwritten rules, power dynamics, and covert agendas that exist in the workplace.

Creating a network of connections amongst the various divisions and tiers of the company is one useful tactic. Through fostering relationships and utilizing social capital, people can obtain important knowledge, assets, and chances. Office politics must be approached ethically, nevertheless, to make sure that power is used for the benefit of society as a whole rather than for individual benefit.

12.2.6 Ethical Aspects of Influence at Work

Even though subtle persuasion tactics can be very effective in the workplace, one must always think about the moral ramifications of their choices. Maintaining a balance between one's own interests and the organization's and its members' overall welfare is necessary for ethical influence.

People ought to make an effort to use their power in a way that upholds justice, openness, and respect for others. It is best to stay away from manipulative strategies, coercion, and unethical behavior since they can destroy relationships, undermine trust, and have long-lasting bad effects.

Individuals can manage power dynamics, form alliances, and accomplish their goals while upholding their integrity and ethical standards in the workplace by being skilled at the art of subtle influence. The power dance in the workplace is delicate, but people can master it with the correct tactics and a thorough grasp of human psychology. This will have a long-lasting effect on their careers and the organizations they work for.

12.3 Using Persuasion in Social and Public Contexts

We have discussed the nuances of subtle influence in interpersonal and professional settings in earlier chapters. Let's now shift our focus to public and social contexts, where the influence of dance takes on a distinct shape. Subtle influence can be a useful tool for navigating surroundings and accomplishing goals in a variety of settings, including public events, social gatherings, and community organizations.

12.3.1 Comprehending the Public Influence Dynamics

People in public spaces tend to be diverse, with a wide range of interests, viewpoints, and driving forces. It is essential to comprehend the dynamics at work and modify your strategy in order to exert influence in these circumstances.

12.3.1.1 Recognizing Opinion Leaders and Important Players

Public contexts have their own power structures and powerful people, just like in organizational politics. Finding these important figures and thought leaders can help you gain important insights into social dynamics and place yourself in a position of power. Those with large followings, deep networks, or positions of authority should be taken notice of. By establishing a rapport with these people, you can take advantage of their influence to achieve your own goals.

12.3.1.2   Establishing   social   capital
Social capital is frequently the unit of exchange for influence in public and social contexts. The networks, connections, and relationships that people possess and may use to influence and win over others are referred to as social capital. Developing real connections, actively interacting with people, and giving back to the community or social group are all part of building social capital. Your power to influence others will increase if you put in the time and effort to develop your social capital and position yourself as a recognized and trustworthy member of the community.

12.3.2 The Art of Convincing in Public
The art of persuasion becomes crucial in public contexts. The capacity to persuade others is crucial, whether you're trying to change public opinion, get support for a project, or advocate for a cause. Here are some tactics to think about:

12.3.2.1 Developing Strong Sentences

Create messages that connect with your audience if you want to influence people in public. Make sure your message is in line with their values, worldview, and areas of interest, and convey your points in an engaging way. To emotionally connect your audience and leave them with a lasting impression, use storytelling strategies. You may present your message in a way that appeals to your audience and raises the possibility that they will be influenced by your thoughts by getting to know their needs and desires.

12.3.2.2 Forming Coalitions and Alliances

The strength of group influence in public spaces should not be undervalued. You can boost your influence and the likelihood that your goals will be met by forming coalitions and alliances with like-minded people or groups. Find people or organizations that share your objectives and principles, then cooperate to present a unified front. Through combining resources, exchanging knowledge, and organizing work, you can have a bigger effect and raise your chances of success.

12.3.3 Ethical Factors in Public Persuasion

Applying subtle influence in public and social situations requires careful consideration of ethical issues, just like any other form of influence. It is crucial to make sure that your activities support the greater good, do no harm to others, and are consistent with your values. The following are some moral things to remember:

12.3.3.1 Openness and sincerity
To establish credibility and trust, you must always act with honesty and integrity in your dealings. If you want to accomplish your goals, don't use deceit or manipulation. Instead, be honest about your plans and motivations. You may build a reputation for being a trustworthy person and make others more open to your influence by being open and truthful.

12.3.3.2 Honoring Various Points of View
Diverse viewpoints and beliefs are frequently evident in public spaces. When using influence, it is crucial to respect and take into account these different points of view. Instead of discounting or ignoring different viewpoints, have a productive conversation and look for areas of agreement. Respecting different points of view will help you create a more welcoming and cooperative atmosphere, which will increase the likelihood that positive results will be reached.

12.3.4 The Durability of Subtle Influence in Public Places

Your social and public influence can have a long-lasting effect on people, communities, and society at large. You can influence public opinion, promote good change, and advance societal progress by strategically and ethically using subtle influence. Recall that having influence extends beyond self-interest to include having a positive influence on the environment.

In conclusion, using influence in social and public contexts necessitates a dedication to ethical issues, a thorough comprehension of the processes at work, and the capacity to create messages that are compelling. You may move through public spaces with grace, accomplish your goals, and make a lastiny impression on the people around you if you can become an expert in the art of subtle influence in these situations.

12.4 The Subtle Influence's Lasting Effect
When it comes to subtle influence, our acts can have an effect that lasts far longer than the instant they occur. Relationships, organizations, and even societies may be shaped by the waves we generate via our interactions. For people who want to become experts in the field and use it properly, it is imperative to comprehend the long-term effects of subtle influence.

12.4.1 Fostering enduring connections
The development of enduring relationships is one of the most important components of subtle influence. We provide the groundwork for enduring relationships that stand the test of time by fostering rapport, trust, and respect for one another. These connections serve as a source of influence, cooperation, and support that makes it easier for us to deal with life's challenges.

Our influence lasts longer when we approach relationships with sincerity and integrity. Individuals whom people respect and trust have a greater chance of influencing and getting listeners. We position ourselves as people deserving of influence when we continually exhibit our dependability, sensitivity, and expertise. This mutual respect and trust can go beyond the brief exchange, leaving a lasting impression on how other people see and react to us.

12.4.2 Molding the Culture of the Organization
Organizational cultures can be significantly impacted by subtle influences as well. We may encourage people to follow our example by living up to the ideals and standards we want to see in the workplace. The way individuals interact, make decisions, and approach their work inside the business is shaped by our actions, attitudes, and behaviors.

Leading by example and constantly exhibiting the traits we want to see in others causes a domino effect that spreads throughout the entire organization. The norms, values, and beliefs that direct the group's collective behavior can be shaped by our influence. Through the cultivation of a collaborative culture, transparent communication, and moral decision-making, we establish an atmosphere that stimulates development, novelty, and achievement.

12.4.3 Motivating Shift and Adjustment
It is possible to bring about change and transformation in society as well as in

individuals through subtle influence. We can adapt our influence to meet the requirements of others by being aware of their motives, ambitions, and aspirations. Strategic communication, attentive listening, and empathy are powerful tools that we may use to sow the seeds of change in the hearts and minds of people around us.

The improvement of society as a whole occurs when we use our influence to encourage constructive change. We have the power to influence history by standing up to the status quo, challenging dated notions, and supporting innovative ideas. The way that people, communities, and even entire nations are changing is evidence of human influence's long-lasting effects.

12.4.4 Bequests and Legacies
We can leave a lasting legacy that lasts longer than our own lives by mastering the art of subtle influence. We make sure that our impact continues to shape the world long after we are gone by passing on our knowledge, wisdom, and values to future generations. We can inspire others to continue the tradition of subtle influence by sharing the lessons we have learned through writing, teaching, or mentoring.

Our legacy is shaped by both the material accomplishments we leave behind and the intangible effects we have on other people's lives. Our ability to uplift and impact individuals around us shapes their own experiences by influencing their viewpoints, decisions, and behaviors. Our influence continues in this way, sustaining a cycle of development and progress.

12.4.5 Subtle Influence's Responsibilities tremendous power with a tremendous deal of responsibility. It is critical for us to understand the moral ramifications of our acts as practitioners of subtle influence. Depending on how we choose to use our influence, it can have a lasting beneficial or negative effect. It is our responsibility to make sure that the values of justice, fairness, and the greater good are reflected in the impact we have.

We may use our influence responsibly and ethically by thinking through the effects of what we do and making an effort to do the least amount of harm possible. Unintended effects are a possibility, and we must actively seek to reduce them. By means of introspection, ongoing education, and a dedication to individual development, we can skillfully and compassionately maneuver through the shadows of influence.

In summary, subtle influence has a wide-ranging and complex long-term effect. It leaves a legacy and molds organizations, civilizations, and interpersonal relationships. It also inspires change. As we maneuver through the dance of power, let us not lose sight of our enormous influence and the accompanying accountability. We can make an everlasting impression that uplifts everyone around us and endures beyond time by becoming experts at the art of subtle influence.